MISSION
VISION
PASSION

To Karen

Neh 4:14

Roy Benyamin

MISSION VISION PASSION

LEADERSHIP LESSONS IN NEHEMIAH

ROY BENJAMIN

XULON PRESS

Xulon Press
2301 Lucien Way #415
Maitland, FL 32751
407.339.4217
www.xulonpress.com

Unless otherwise indicated, cripture quotations taken from the Holy Bible, New International Version (NIV). Copyright © 1978 by New York International Bible Society. Used by permission. All rights reserved.

Scripture quotations taken from the King James Version (KJV) – *public domain.*

Edited by Xulon Press

Printed in the United States of America.

ISBN-13: 978-1-54561-354-2

CONTENTS

Part 3: PASSION 119

INTRODUCTION

I came to an understanding of missions very early as a young boy growing up on a tiny Caribbean island which was then a colony of Britain. I attended a church that was started by British missionaries and they had an early influence on my life and many of the skills I learned, were taught to me by these missionaries.

In addition to establishing churches, they were also involved in the community, and as they performed their mission work, they invited us to assist them in their various projects. I saw these missionaries not only as preachers but as people with multiple skills who could help us solve the everyday problems we faced. I don't believe these men and women had formal training for the things they did because they had traveled from Britain to the Caribbean to preach the gospel and help start churches. However, once they got to our tiny island that was underdeveloped at that time, they realized that their mission work was going to involve a lot more than what they initially signed up for.

They became integrated into the social and cultural fabric of the island where they lived and worked tirelessly for many years until their death. For them, this was the mission they were called to and they were fully committed to it and I learned some very important life lessons from these missionaries.

They were men and women of the Bible and they were diligent in presenting it at church. They also got us interested in reading the Bible as well as being able to have a good knowledge of it. They gave us books and study guides to help us with our Bible studies and lessons and they helped us to get a true meaning and understanding of the Bible. Because of their efforts, I became an enthusiastic student of the Bible.

Not only were they preachers of the word but they were doers of the word. They helped many individuals who were poor by giving them food, money, and clothing. The female missionaries initiated skills-training classes for the women that would help them learn skills they could eventually use to get a job or be self-employed. I understood very early, the power of enabling people, and learned how to work hard at the things that would help me later in life.

I learned how to be a man of integrity from watching these preachers and seeing how they conducted their lives. They were upright and honest and they were good examples for us to follow. They demonstrated lives that was pleasing to God and they taught me how to lead. Later, when I became one of the first local leaders to succeed them in the leadership of the church, they supported and encouraged me in my work. As I watched them doing their missionary work, I was inspired by their service and it challenged me to be a committed Christian worker.

I was personally impacted by one of the missionaries as he baptized me as a young boy, performed my wedding ceremony, dedicated both of my babies and he was there through the significant moments of my life. He has died and gone home to glory, but I still remember his life and work.

Mission work has been going on for a very long time and people who live in developed countries are challenged through a mission's sermon appeal at their local church or some other mission event. They responded to the call of God to take the Gospel message to people in foreign places around the world that either had not heard the message or had a very limited understanding of what that message was. Missionary organizations were set up to sponsor and send missionaries to what was then called the mission field. They were tasked with providing financial and logistical support to these missionaries while they were out in the field and served as a support system and a contact point for them and their families.

One of the most outstanding mission projects is found in the Old Testament, book of Nehemiah. This is a story that all mission organizations should include as an essential part of their mission training for there are many lessons we all can learn from this man and his mission, vision, and passion. Leaders can learn from it and gain tremendous insight from his journey, the way he managed the mission and dealt with the crises that he faced in the various phases. It is interesting to see how he got the people to not only buy into his mission, but to stand with him all the way and help to bring it to completion.

We recently walked through the book of Nehemiah at our men's Bible study and I had read it many times, and done studies on the text. However, I was impacted by the story and its meaning for our times as it shows how we can make a difference in our community and the world at large. I trust that you will be encouraged and blessed by reading this book also.

PART 1 MISSION

1
THE BIRTH
OF A MISSION

Nehemiah came to Persia as a Jewish exile and eventually became a prominent official in the king's palace. He was in a seemingly comfortable position and apparently doing well serving as the wine steward for the king. However, his mind was always on Jerusalem and the situation there. Although he heard some stories from people he talked with, he never really got a detailed report of what was going on.

The opportunity came when his brother, Hanani, arrived from Judah with a group of men. Nehemiah arranged a meeting with them so that he could get a firsthand account of what was happening back in the homeland. He wanted to get to the heart of the matter, so it was not just a casual question of "how is everyone doing at home?" He wanted a true picture and he asked them to give a detailed report. It was a serious question that got a serious reply and the report they gave was clear and comprehensive:

> The people were experiencing suffering and humiliation;

The walls of Jerusalem were still broken down;

The gates had not been restored since they were burned;

There were brokenness, destruction, and deterioration.

The news was not good and Nehemiah was so devastated that he left the meeting and wept bitterly. He was so moved by what he heard that he mourned for several days and did not eat. He realized the gravity of the situation but he also knew that something had to be done. This was a major crisis as the walls were broken and needed not just repair, but restoration and renewal. A major project would have to be undertaken to fix the situation.

It really hit hard but it caused him to think about the root cause and how things got to that place. Before he could do anything about it, he had to determine why it broke and what the contributing factors were that led to the breakdown. When this happens, it helps to ensure that the solution is effective, long-lasting, and that the problem will not be repeated.

Nehemiah dug deep and came up with the root cause of the condition:

The people were living in a sinful state;

There was corruption throughout the land;

They had not kept the commandments of God.

God had stated very clearly to His people "If you transgress, I will scatter you abroad among the nations but if you return to me and keep my commands, I will bring you to the place that I have chosen to set my name." (Nehemiah 1:8-9 NIV) What happened had a direct relationship to what they had done and what God said would be the result.

As Nehemiah prayed and sought for answers, he realized that it was not just the people who had done wrong but that his father's house was also involved. This caused him to understand that if he was part of the problem, he had to be part of the solution.

We learn from Nehemiah that decisions like these are made because of a deep conviction from the heart that if it is going to be done, it must start with me. This mission began with a clear understanding of the situation and a willing spirit and open heart, combined with a strong resolve to do something about it. It will not help the situation in any way just to discuss it and talk about it and not act. He did not have a meeting with the men to brainstorm and come up with ideas about how they could solve the problem. He took personal ownership of the issue and decided that he would travel to Jerusalem and rebuild the wall.

Once he made the decision to begin the mission, he looked to God for direction as to what to do and how to go about doing it. This is a critical component for any mission to be successful for, even with the greatest plan and the best people involved, if God is not directing the mission, it is more likely to go off track. We should seek to partner with God in the things we do because He is the one who knows the future and can guide us through all the complexities and the difficulties that will arise. The key to a successful mission is to let God be the leader and we just follow His leading.

2
MISSION PROMISE

Nehemiah was going over all the things that were happening to the Jews and the condition of the city. He had a vision of the restoration of the city that was in ruins and that God had promised to bring His people together again. This became the driving force behind his desire to rebuild so he reached out to God and reminded Him of His promise to restore His people.

> Remember the instruction you gave your servant Moses, saying, 'If you are unfaithful, I will scatter you among the nations, but if you return to me and obey my commands, then even if your exiled people are at the farthest horizon, I will gather them from there and bring them to the place I have chosen as a dwelling for my Name. (Neh.1:8–9 NIV)

Nehemiah knew that God had promised to return His people from captivity and restore the land, and he was holding Him to His word. The people may have been unfaithful but God is faithful and he trusted the word of God and the faithfulness of God. Having read the word that God outlined to His servant Moses, he knew it in his heart and learned the following things about God.

God' Nature

Nehemiah understood God's nature to restore and that He is a restoring God

> When all these blessings and curses I have set before you come on you and you take them to heart wherever the Lord your God disperses you among the nations, and when you and your children return to the Lord your God and obey Him with all your heart and with all your soul according to everything I command you today, then the Lord your God will restore your fortunes and have compassion on you and gather you again from all the nations where He scattered you. Even if you have been banished to the most distant land under the heavens, from there the Lord your God will gather you and bring you back. (Deut. 30:1–4 NIV)

God's Method

Nehemiah had an insight into what was possible with God and that He could bring change and

transformation to the hearts of the people and cause them to obey and follow Him

> He will bring you to the land that belonged to your ancestors, and you will take possession of it. He will make you more prosperous and numerous than your ancestors. The Lord your God will circumcise your hearts and the hearts of your descendants, so that you may love Him with all your heart and with all your soul, and live. The Lord your God will put all these curses on your enemies who hate and persecute you. You will again obey the Lord and follow all His commands I am giving you today. (Deut. 30:5–8 NIV)

God's Provision

Nehemiah came to the realization that "how" is never a problem with God and that He will always make a way and provide for His people

> Then the Lord your God will make you most prosperous in all the work of your hands and in the fruit of your womb, the young of your livestock and the crops of your land. The Lord will again delight in you and make you prosperous, just as He delighted in your ancestors, if you obey the Lord your God and keep His

commands and decrees that are written
in this Book of the Law and turn to the
Lord your God with all your heart and
with all your soul. (Deut. 30:9–10 NIV)

As you go about your mission work you must also
remember that God has promised to bring salvation
and to restore people's lives. You must believe that
God will be true to His promise and that whatever He
said will come to pass. Hold on to His promises and
watch Him work in the lives of the people you care
about. Here are some lessons that you can learn from
Nehemiah's trust in God's promises.

God is able to save and His salvation is absolute

Therefore, He is able to save completely,
those who come to God through Him,
because He always lives to intercede
for them. (Hebrews 7:25 NIV)

God has a plan for all who believe in Him and He will
deliver His people

Do not let your hearts be troubled. You
believe in God; believe also in me. My
Father's house has many rooms; if that
were not so, would I have told you that
I am going there to prepare a place for
you? And if I go and prepare a place for
you, I will come back and take you to be
with me that you also may be where I
am. (John 14:1–3 NIV)

God wants all people to come to Him so He can relieve them from the weight of sin they carry

> Come to me, all you who are weary and burdened, and I will give you rest. Take my yoke upon you and learn from me, for I am gentle and humble in heart, and you will find rest for your souls. For my yoke is easy and my burden is light. (Matt. 11:28–29 NIV)

God loves people and He died to save them so that they could come to Him

> For God so loved the world that He gave his one and only Son, that whoever believes in Him shall not perish but have eternal life. For God did not send His Son into the world to condemn the world, but to save the world through Him. Whoever believes in Him is not condemned, but whoever does not believe stands condemned already because they have not believed in the name of God's one and only Son.
>
> This is the verdict: Light has come into the world, but people loved darkness instead of light because their deeds were evil. Everyone who does evil hates the light, and will not come into the light for fear that their deeds will be exposed. But whoever lives by the truth comes

into the light, so that it may be seen plainly that what they have done has been done in the sight of God. (John 3:16–21 NIV)

3
MISSION AND POSITION

A mission that emerges from personal experiences of frustration and pain is very compelling. When the root of the mission is strong enough, it can change people who are sad, disappointed and broken and turn them into dynamic engines that are ready to fight, build, restore or do whatever it takes to bring things back to order.

A mission can be very demanding and forces us to turn within ourselves and examine what we are doing and ask if it is enough. It makes us unwilling to simply stand by and be just an onlooker or a casual observer of the chaos, confusion, and devastation around us.

It makes us dig deep into our souls and causes us to conclude that, as uncomfortable as it may be, something must be done to change the existing circumstances. We cannot accept things as they are and just simply conclude that that's the way it is. We come to understand that if we fail to act on what we know, we will be unfulfilled and empty because we have not reached and achieved our highest purpose.

This is what gripped Nehemiah because he had a great position in the king's palace but there was a calling that had now superseded this position and he knew he must accept the challenge to step up and step out, to make a sacrifice and take some big risks. The thought of this overwhelmed him daily and weighed upon him heavily so that the joy that he once had in service to the king was replaced by the driving force of this mission. There was a voice inside that was calling him to a higher position and he could not shake it for it consumed every area of his being. There was also the vision of the broken wall and the need for it to be rebuilt. It captured his imagination, went deep down into his spirit and the power of the mission was now so much greater than the position.

He had never been sad in the king's presence before, and the call of this mission was hanging on to him and it was very strong and could not be ignored. He was concerned that the king would take notice and become aware that something was wrong and this could cause a problem for him. There was a conflict that had developed between his position and his mission because his position was tied to his duty to the king as his cupbearer and trusted confidante. However, there was something going on that was tugging at his heart and his desire for the mission outweighed his desire to be a cupbearer.

The call to this mission was moving him away from his position and he was scared because the position was prestigious and had great perks and benefits and it was a job he enjoyed. He performed his duties with distinction, and as a key person in the king's inner circle, he had every reason to be conflicted and disturbed. The king depended on him and moving away from the position could be considered as a sign of disloyalty or betrayal. The results could be devastating because the king's business was very important and there was no place for people who were not committed to his service.

Many of you right now are experiencing similar situations as you are in great positions that provide you with a great compensation and comes with a benefits package. The opportunities are phenomenal and you are nice and comfortable, or so it seems. Suddenly, during your daily routine, a call to mission comes to you because mission calls are unreasonable and have no sense of timing or schedule. When the call comes, it can often be disruptive and seems to come at the wrong time for it causes you to think long and hard, it brings feelings of fear, uncertainty, and doubt. Because of this, there are many people who choose to go on with their ordinary lives, serving in positions where they are unhappy and choosing to go on accepting a title or position that does not have their future in mind.

You cannot keep on doing what you've always done and simply stand by and do nothing about it because if you reject the call to mission, you will fall backward into flatness and emptiness despite the things the position offers. I'm not saying that this applies to everyone as we all have our various callings in life and where you are presently may be the place where God intends for you to be. My point is, if God has been tugging at your heart and there has been a clear call to a mission, you must obey the call and be willing to make the sacrifice. You must also be willing to endure the times when you must live with less while you move on to fulfill the mission for it will be rewarding and fulfilling in the end.

4
MISSION READINESS

N ehemiah accepted the call and was now ready for the mission and it required him to spend a lot of time going over all the various aspects of the project. There was a lot of planning and logistics involved, and he was now moving from being a cupbearer to a strategic planner. A mission will stretch you and bend you and it will take you from being ordinary to extraordinary. There will be areas where you will encounter situations for which you have no training or background experience, but God will give you the wisdom and ability to do it.

We discussed the conflict between position and mission but there are also times when the position will prepare you for the mission. Nehemiah was strategically placed in a position that would eventually help to facilitate the mission. His job as a cupbearer gave him access to the king as well as the resources he would need to build the wall. If he had been a regular worker in the fields harvesting grain, it would be nearly impossible to even consider a mission of this magnitude for he would not have the connections or the resources available.

He was being trained for this mission and the time spent working in the palace contributed greatly to the training process. This was the right place to gather a wide range of experience in becoming a servant leader and it helped him to understand many things that he would not have learned elsewhere.

Schools and educational institutions should be places that address the student's need for well-placed learning. They gain experiences with a program that speaks strongly to their ability to solve problems, make intelligent decisions, and get them motivated to learn and grow. Our young people must learn not to be afraid of knowledge or turn away from opportunities to learn. They should take responsibility for their own learning and with the help of their teachers, develop new skills and abilities. However, I also believe that real world experiences can help a person gain knowledge that will remain with them throughout their lifetime. Internships and summer work programs are great opportunities for this.

Nehemiah was not at a summer program but in a real job with real responsibilities and would soon find out that he needed all the things that could be learned on the job. Life is a university of real learning and we all should be eager students and learn all we can while we can.

There is no record of the timeline between the time he got the call to build the wall and the actual start time of building. It seemed to be a significant time span, but Nehemiah did not just sit around and wait for the time to go by. He used the time wisely and devoted himself to preparation, which involved a lot of planning, and he spent many hours in prayer. These were the key components that would help not only to get the project started but to see it completed.

5

PREPARATION FOR THE MISSION

P reparation time is always the most difficult part of a project. However, the amount of time and effort that goes into the preparation stage will help to determine the success or failure of the project. Preparation is laying the framework for the project and requires a lot of thought and insight. Before construction takes place on any building, all the stakeholders share their ideas of what it should look like, its capabilities and function as well as its capacity. These thoughts and ideas are then converted into a blueprint mapped out by an architect. A series of meetings for review and approval are held before construction, and this happens over a period of months, sometimes years.

Preparation for mission takes time and maybe God has been at work in your life for quite a while getting you ready for that which He is calling you to. The job you do, the people you meet, opportunities that come your way and even the difficulties, tests and trials are all part of the preparation to get you mission ready.

A church or ministry must be prepared for what God wants to do in their congregation or organization. The leadership should set spiritual goals for growth both numerically and spiritually as they seek to follow God's vision for the future and where He would like to take His people. Preparation for service requires a changed mindset and a commitment to arise from the apathy and complacency to the mission that God has set for His church. The mission is to preach the gospel to the whole world and make disciples of all people and help them to experience the life God intended for them.

This will require taking risks and making sacrifices and can cause some discomfort because change and growth are not easy and it takes time and patience. However, the rewards will be great as you see people's lives changed, the community transformed and the ministry blessed for its dedicated service to God and His people.

When a person enlists in the military, they must go through boot camp before they can even get to their place of service. This gives them some experience of what things could be like on the battlefield if they ever were to be called to combat and it helps to prepare them for war.

Nehemiah did his work of preparation and it was obvious from his response to the king. When he was asked what was troubling him and what exactly he wanted, he did not have to stop to think about it or tell the king he would get back to him later. The answer was clear and precise and he outlined what was happening, what he intended to do, and what he would need to facilitate the mission that was laid on his heart.

Where are you in the preparation process? I know you have big ideas and would like to accomplish great things. However, before you can do all these things, you will have to go through a time of preparation. God will enable you for service in the new mission but He wants you to be prepared.

Guidelines for the Preparation Plan

You must always be in a state of readiness for the mission because preparation requires vigilance and watchfulness.

> Be dressed ready for service and keep your lamps burning. (Luke 12:35 NIV)

A mission requires detailed preparation so you must have all the things in place and be ready to go at the first call

> This is how you are to eat it: with your cloak tucked into your belt, your sandals on your feet and your staff in your hand. Eat it in haste; it is the Lord's Passover. (Exod. 12:11 NIV)

Mental preparation is very important and your mind must be alert and ready to think clearly

> Therefore, prepare your minds for action, keep sober in spirit, fix your hope completely on the grace to be brought to

you at the revelation of Jesus Christ. (1
Pet. 1:13 NIV)

As you prepare for the mission, you must also be prepared to fight because the people who oppose the
mission will come against you to stop the work that
God has given you to do

> About forty thousand armed for battle
> crossed over before the Lord to the
> plains of Jericho for war. (Josh. 4:13 NIV)

Mapping and documentation is a vital part of preparing
for the mission because it gives everyone involved a
clear picture of what is involved

> As the men started on their way to map
> out the land, Joshua instructed them,
> "Go and make a survey of the land and
> write a description of it. Then return
> to me, and I will cast lots for you here
> at Shiloh in the presence of the Lord."
> (Josh. 18:8 NIV)

You must have faith to believe God even when it
seems impossible from a human perspective. Know
that God is behind the scenes working it out and He
calls you to trust and believe in His ability to come
through for you

> By faith Noah, when warned about
> things not yet seen, in holy fear built an
> ark to save his family. By his faith he

condemned the world and became heir of the righteousness that is in keeping with faith. (Heb. 11:7 NIV)

God has already prepared for you, He has everything in place just waiting for you

If they had been thinking of the country they had left, they would have had opportunity to return. Instead, they were longing for a better country—a heavenly one. Therefore, God is not ashamed to be called their God, for He has prepared a city for them. (Heb. 11:16 NIV)

6
PLANNING FOR THE MISSION

Nehemiah was not in any doubt as to the extent of the project because Hanani and the other men had given him a clear description of the damage that had been done and he knew it was going to take a lot to bring things back to order.

To accomplish this rebuilding and restoration project, a lot of planning had to be done. There were many things that had to be taken into consideration, not only in terms of logistics but supplies and manpower. At that time, he had not thought about security plans as that was not an issue at the time. However, he could include it later because he had a master plan in place and he was able to factor in the security details as it became necessary.

The Bible talks a lot about planning and the importance of it. Jesus emphasized this in His sermon:

> Suppose one of you wants to build a tower. Won't you first sit down and estimate the cost to see if you have enough money to complete it? For if you lay the foundation and are not able to finish it,

everyone who sees it will ridicule you, saying, "This person began to build and wasn't able to finish." Or suppose a king is about to go to war against another king. Won't he first sit down and consider whether he is able with ten thousand men to oppose the one coming against him with twenty thousand? If he is not able, he will send a delegation while the other is still a long way off and will ask for terms of peace. (Luke 14: 28–32 NIV)

The message of Jesus in these verses is that a certain amount of planning must take place before you go about doing things and you must be diligent in the planning process. Jesus thought that it was important to plan and you must also give high priority to planning in your personal lives, business, and ministry.

A plan gives you some form of guidance and sets out a path for you to follow. Although planning can be tedious and sometimes boring, once the plan is in place, you then know where you are going and have some idea where you will end up.

The plan Nehemiah put together outlined all the supplies he would need for the building. He knew he would need passage letters as he journeyed through foreign territory as well as order letters for the timber. He had a time schedule in place so when the king asked for his travel plans, he knew the estimated length of the project as he had it included in his master plan.

We need to see more planning coming from our churches and ministries. The time has come for us to rethink what we are doing and where we are going and set meaningful and realistic goals for the work we are engaged in. As we make our plans, commit them to the Lord for His guidance for, if we fail to plan then we are setting ourselves up for failure in the work of the ministry.

Guidelines for Mission Planning

God has a plan for you and He has outlined it

> "For I know the plans I have for you," declares the Lord, "plans to prosper you and not to harm you, plans to give you hope and a future. Then you will call on me and come and pray to me, and I will listen to you. You will seek me and find me when you seek me with all your heart." (Jer. 29:11–13 NIV).

God already knows the plans He has for your ministry and He is asking you to do four things: call on Him, come to Him, pray to Him and seek Him with all your heart. It is God's mission and therefore, you must seek to understand His plan for the mission and His will for the mission.

When you get an understanding of the plan, you must then follow the plan. God is the one who placed the dream in your heart and you must not be afraid of the size of the mission because it seems too big for the staff and the budget. You must be bold and approach the mission with confidence, knowing that He who began a good work in you will carry it on to completion until the day of Jesus Christ. (Phil. 1:6 NIV).

God has a purpose for you and He will reveal it as you submit your plans to Him

> "Many are the plans in a person's heart, but it is the Lord's purpose that prevails (Prov. 19:21 NIV)."

God wants you to bring your plans to Him and He will take care of them

> "Commit to the Lord whatever you do, and He will establish your plans (Prov. 16:3 NIV)."

God will equip you to carry out the mission

> Now may the God of peace, who through the blood of the eternal covenant brought back from the dead our Lord Jesus, that great Shepherd of the sheep, equip you with everything good for doing His will, and may He work in us what is pleasing to Him, through Jesus Christ, to whom be glory for ever and ever. (Heb. 13: 20–21 NIV)

God has all that you need for the mission and He has already supplied the things that are necessary.

God will give you wisdom to not only understand the plan but to execute the plan

"If any of you lacks wisdom, you should ask God, who gives generously to all without finding fault, and it will be given to you (James 1:5 NIV)." There are times when you get to a roadblock and seem to hit a wall in the planning process but it is then you can trust God for direction

> Trust in the Lord with all your heart, and lean not on your own understanding; In all your ways acknowledge Him, and He shall direct your paths. (Prov. 3:5–6 KJV)"

It is God's plan for His kingdom to be manifested here on earth and as His Kingdom people, you are entrusted to help establish His Kingdom as part of the mission plan.

> "Your kingdom come, your will be done, on earth as it is in heaven (Matt. 6:10 NIV)."

The planning stage is long and hard but be encouraged and persevere to the end

> "You need to persevere so that when you have done the will of God, you will

receive what He has promised (Heb. 10:36 NIV)."

The planning process will come to a successful completion as we allow God to lead and guide us

"The Lord works out everything to its proper end (Prov. 16:4 NIV)."

7
PRAYING FOR
THE MISSION

When Nehemiah got the news, his first response was to pray. He turned to God in his time of distress and grief and his approach indicated that this was his regular practice and not just a quick, get-out-of-trouble prayer. It is evident that he had constant communion with God and this was what he did when things became tough. In his prayer, he indicated that he was praying day and night, signifying he had an ongoing, constant relationship with God and prayed to Him about every situation he faced. It was through the prayer that God spoke to him about going to Jerusalem to rebuild the wall. Once that call became clear to him, he then prayed for success and favor from the king. When he appeared before the king, he was nervous about the situation he was facing, so he reached out and prayed to the God of Heaven. There is a definite pattern here and it is consistent throughout the book for as he got more involved in the project, he always turned to God first when he faced difficult times.

The other important lesson to learn from his prayer is his humility before God and his spirit of repentance. He wasn't trying to make a deal with God or to coerce Him into doing something special for him or his people.

He identified their transgressions, confessed that they were wrong to disobey and turn from His laws and acknowledged that the situation they now faced in Jerusalem was a result of disobedience. He recognized God as forgiving and merciful and that He would help his people if they repented. You can have the best plan and spend a lot of time in preparation but if you do not pray, your projects are likely to fail.

When I was growing up, the church I attended had a designated night every week for prayer meeting. All the saints would gather together and pray for the needs of the church, the community, individuals who were facing difficulties and families that were in need. They considered this to be an important part of the life of the church and over time there were many answered prayers.

In our day, we see a lot of time given for programs, celebrations, and festivities. We hear prayer requests being read out but I'm not sure how much time is given in the weekly service calendar for corporate prayer. I'm not knocking anybody's services but this is an indication of the power of the church in our day. The saints prayed because they believed that where there are constant prayer and intercession, there will be great power and where there is a lack of prayer, there will be a lack of power.

We live in a fast-paced, high-speed environment where everyone is on a time schedule. Before you step out to your daily work and mission, you must pray to the God of heaven for direction, wisdom, and guidance as well as provision and protection. The tendency is that you pray when you run into a wall and cannot go any further or a crisis happens, then you call for an emergency prayer meeting to help get out of trouble.

I believe the time has come to return to the prayer meetings of days gone by where people would cry out to the Lord and ask for His help before they did anything or started a project.

Nehemiah made a repeated statement throughout the book, "so I prayed to the Lord of heaven." I am convinced that if we have more prayer, we would have more power.

Guidelines for Prayer Planning

Be assured that whenever you go to God in prayer, He hears you and will respond accordingly

> This is the confidence we have in approaching God: that if we ask anything according to His will, He hears us. And if we know that He hears us, whatever we ask, we know that we have what we asked of Him. (1John 5:15–16 NIV)

You must go to God trusting and believing and know that you will receive that which you ask for in His name

"Therefore, I tell you, whatever you ask for in prayer, believe that you have received it, and it will be yours (Mark 11:24 NIV)."

God has good things in store for you and He will give good gifts to you

If you, then, though you are evil, know how to give good gifts to your children, how much more will your Father in heaven give good gifts to those who ask Him! (Matt. 7:11 NIV)

Even when it looks like nothing is happening, you must be persistent in your prayer to God "Then Jesus told His disciples a parable to show them that they should always pray and not give up (Luke 18:1 NIV)."

When you pray, you must come to God with confidence, knowing that He is touched by your needs and will answer your prayer

Seeing then that we have a great high priest, that is passed into the heavens, Jesus the Son of God, let us hold fast our profession. For we have not a high priest which cannot be touched with the feeling of our infirmities; but was in all points tempted like as we are, yet without sin. Let us therefore come boldly unto the throne of grace, that we may

obtain mercy, and find grace to help in
time of need. (Heb. 4: 15–16 KJV)

You must not rely on your own strength or power but
rely on God's strength

"Look to the Lord and His strength; seek
His face always (1 Chron. 16:11 NIV)."

God promised that if you pray in humility before Him,
He will hear and answer your prayer

If my people, who are called by my name,
will humble themselves and pray and
seek my face and turn from their wicked
ways, then I will hear from heaven, and
I will forgive their sin and will heal their
land. Now my eyes will be open and my
ears attentive to the prayers offered in
this place. (2 Chron. 7:14–15 NIV)

God is attentive to your prayers and is available to
you at all times

Then you will call on me and come
and pray to me, and I will listen to you.
You will seek me and find me when
you seek me with all your heart. (Jer.
29:12–13 NIV)

God invites you to call unto Him and He will reveal
great and mighty things to you

"Call to me and I will answer you and tell you great and unsearchable things you do not know (Jer. 33:3 NIV)."

8
MAKING THE MISSION POSSIBLE

Once Nehemiah had prepared, planned, and prayed, it was time to get the mission going. His first order of business was to talk to the king about his mission and let him know what was on his mind and what he was about to do. As a trusted servant and an important officer in the palace, he needed to have the king's permission and blessing for the project. The way he presented his case for going on this mission, would help to determine the support he would get and how much the king would be willing to contribute to the project. If he came across rude and arrogant and demanded the king let him go because this was a mission from God, it would not go well.

There is a lesson here for those of you who are in jobs or other situations where you feel the need to move on. How you move on is just as important as where and what you are moving to, and you should try as hard as you possibly can, to leave your positions in good standing. You must not burn bridges or destroy the goodwill that was built over time because you may move away from the position but the "stuff" you accumulate, will also move with you and can greatly affect your mission. Your call to mission requires you to have a mission mindset, which means that you should try to be free from the conflicts and confusion that would eventually weigh you down and become a hindrance as you move onward and forward to the mission. Pray for whatever situation you are facing and ask God to give you favor with the people you work with and those you work for. You cannot allow ongoing feuds and fights to hold you back. Leave your position in good standing and go strongly toward your mission.

Every good project needs a sponsor that would provide support, and give credibility to the cause. In Nehemiah's case, the ideal sponsor was the king himself and he asked God to give him favor with him and his prayer was answered. God worked on the king's heart and caused him to agree to give Nehemiah leave for the project as well as supplies and materials for the building of the wall. In his meeting with the king, he was given an opportunity to ask for what he needed and because of his preparation and planning, he already had a list of all the things he would need for the project. This suggests that he had a project plan as well as a logistics plan. He had done all the estimates and had a very good idea of what it would take to build the wall and the city gates. He knew exactly what he wanted to do and when he was asked about the timeline of the project, he could give a time frame although, at that time, he might not have understood about project scope creep. This is where you have a set list of items outlined in the project, but by the time the project gets started, the list expands and the scope of the project expands. You will see this happening later in this project.

The king was a good sponsor and in addition to the supplies, he gave him letters of recommendation, security guards for the journey, and everything he needed to facilitate the mission, so the mission was now possible.

For every mission or project, you will always have stakeholders who have a vested interest and could help to determine the outcome of the project. You need to have a good understanding of those persons and their influence, as that will be key to your success in dealing with them. These are some things you will need to consider as you launch your mission:

You will need to understand the positions of these stakeholders and what power or control they may have over the key areas of your mission. Factors like how long they have been in that position is important, as longevity and seniority could be an indicator of their sphere of influence. You may also want to find out who influences them and who they listen to as they most likely will discuss the project with these people and they can help to sway them one way or the other.

Give them sufficient amount of information to get them interested in your mission and help them see its importance. Nehemiah told the king about the condition of the city and the need to repair it and what would be required to complete the mission. He had the information available and could present it in a way that the king was interested and wanted to support it. If they cannot understand it, they will not support it and they will not feel that they can have a stake in the project. It would be like trying to get the seventy-five-year-old chairman of your deacon's board to support funding for a church database that would include the demographics of your church's neighborhood that your staff will use for an outreach mission. You will have to explain the concept in a simple and easy way that makes sense and show him the benefits of having it and what it would do for the growth of the church.

You will have to determine the best method of communicating with the people who can enable or block your project. Nehemiah had only one way to talk to the king about his mission and that was to stand before him and present his case. However, in our time, there are so many communication channels and it is important to know which method to use for the various people we must interact with as each person has a different preference and it also depends on their status. Imagine, if you sent out a proposal by email to your board and the next day one of the members meet up with the chairman who is very sensitive and difficult to deal with, and he begins to discuss the matter with the chairman who had not read his email and did not see the proposal. He will feel slighted because you did not call and give him notice in advance about the proposal you were about to send out and he decides to block your proposal just for that reason. It is very important to understand the best methods to communicate your ideas and proposals to each stakeholder.

The most important thing to determine is what you will need from the people that you would like to help sponsor your mission. Nehemiah knew exactly what he needed and he also knew the king had all those things so he would be the one to go to and ask for what he needed. Had he gone to the procurement officer in the palace, he might be able to give him some things but anything that was over and above a certain number or cost would have to be approved by the king so the best approach was to go straight to the king who could make it happen. There are three categories of people you will encounter as you seek help for your mission. There are those who are able but not willing, then there are those who are willing but not able and there are some who are both able and willing and you must go to those people to help your mission and give you the things you will need to complete it. Adopt Nehemiah's strategy by asking God to open their heart and give you favor with them, then approach them intelligently and honestly and make your request for assistance.

9
OPPORTUNITIES BRING CHALLENGES

The period between the conception and the start of a project could be long and tedious as it involves planning, meetings, approvals, and implementation. However, once the project is launched, there is a sense of joy and anticipation and the goal is to bring it to completion on time and under budget.

Having spent many years in project management, I know that the feeling of joy and exhilaration at the start of a project can go away fast and can turn instead to anxiety and frustration. I emphasized earlier, the need for planning and preparation and its importance in a project. However, I must be open and honest and let you know that there will be challenges and road-blocks that are unexpected and unwanted. This is all part of the mission and we must always be aware that the enemy will try to hinder the work of God and create setbacks.

Nehemiah came to Jerusalem and performed his site survey, checked out the logistics plan to make sure it was in alignment with the situation on the ground. He held a charter meeting with the project stakeholders and reminded them of the state of the broken walls and gates, and the desolation of the city. He presented his plan to rebuild the wall, gave all the reasons why it should be rebuilt and he got total buy in from the meeting with everyone voting unanimously to start rebuilding.

The next day, the news of the project launch hits the Jerusalem press and when some of the city officials heard about it, they were not happy and decided to visit the project office to talk to Nehemiah. They confronted him and told him that this project was not necessary and strongly voiced their opposition to it, promising to close it down.

What do you do in that situation? These men were officials and obviously, seemed to have the power and influence to shut down the project. Nehemiah replied to them that it was not up to them to decide the success or failure of the project but it was the God of heaven that would cause it to prosper.

How did he know this and could say it with such confidence? It came from his time in prayer where God gave him the assurance that He would be with him and bless the mission. He went on to affirm that the wall would be rebuilt but they would not have any part in the project and he would not consult them or seek favors from their offices.

Nehemiah was very clear about the mission and demonstrated the character strength that is needed in a project leader. The conviction that was driving him to rebuild the wall was deep in his heart, there was no room for fear or compromise and he was not willing to back down or negotiate with these men.

A mission is tenacious and can take hold of you so tightly that you are not allowed to waver or shift even when opposition comes. The commitment to mission will be greater than the ridicule or mocking of the haters and detractors. You must stand and keep fighting the good fight and stay true to your calling to the mission.

In any mission, there will be criticism and opposition but these are some important principles you should follow, outlined below.

The strength of a leader is not just demonstrated in their administrative skills and their ability to prepare, plan and communicate, but it is displayed in the times of the four D's—dissent, disputes, disagreements, and disaster. The leader must not only shine in the good times when all is going well but he will need to stand up and lead when things are down and the mission is at risk.

Dissent

There will always be dissent and opposition in any group or organization and it should not be discouraged or put down because opposition is one of the great pillars of a democratic movement. Any nation that is progressive will always have an opposition group that will not only counter the governing views but will scrutinize its policies and look closely at the laws that are being introduced and implemented. The leader then must always be ready for some form of resistance to the mission and should not take it personally but have the conviction that the mission is of God, seek to get the dissenters to understand the vision and become a part of your team. There will be those who will never be convinced or converted and will make it their mission to shut down your project but you should never give up or give in but keep on working.

Disputes

Whenever a group of people come together, there are going to be disputes which could run deep and threaten the flow of the project. The leader must be on guard for petty disputes arising out of feuding and fighting for rank or titles or personality conflicts. The leader must also decide when to intervene and when to stay out of the fight. There are two examples of this that you can follow how Jesus handled each situation in the book of Luke where He was teaching: "Someone in the crowd cried out in a loud voice and said to him, 'Teacher, tell my brother to divide the inheritance with me.' Jesus replied, 'Man, who appointed me a judge or an arbiter between you (Luke 12:13–14 NIV)?'" He decided not to get involved in a fight between two brothers arguing over the contents of a will in the middle of His teaching to the crowd. He did not get off from His teaching mission to act as a judge in a family court. He told the man that there were qualified judges who could handle that matter and this was not the time or the place to settle a family issue.

There is another story in Luke where he did get involved in a dispute

> As Jesus and His disciples were on their way, He came to a village where a woman named Martha opened her home to Him. She had a sister called Mary, who sat at the Lord's feet listening to what He said. But Martha was distracted by all the preparations that had to be made. She came to Him and asked, "Lord, don't you care that my sister has left me to do the work by myself? Tell her to help me!"
>
> "Martha, Martha," the Lord answered, "you are worried and upset about many things, but few things are needed, or indeed only one. Mary has chosen what is better, and it will not be taken away from her." (Luke 10:38-42 NIV)

Here were two sisters quarreling over chores, and Jesus used this as a teaching opportunity to help them understand the importance of setting priorities and making good choices. This is so important for leaders to learn how to turn disputes into positive lessons.

Disagreements

There will be disagreements that will test your faith and bring out the true strength of your character. Some people will come to your place like these men did to Nehemiah, and tell you straight to your face, they do not agree with what you are doing and will let you know that they will do everything in their power to shut down your project. It is in these times that you will have to be firm and steadfast because their intention is to shake you and get you off course so you will have to stand up to them and declare that the work is of God and you are determined to complete the mission. You must also be sure to follow Nehemiah's example and do not allow them to have any part in your project because their goal is to sabotage and hinder the work. Do not be afraid of disagreements as they will come, but stand strong and do not allow the work to cease.

Disasters

Disasters are also to be expected and you will have to lead your people through them. Nehemiah faced a crisis when the taunts of the enemy escalated to death threats to his workers and his project was in jeopardy. The enemy was planning an attack and it was now time for action and Nehemiah had to dig deep to come up with a strategy that would not only protect the people but also defend the project. He gave them a great word

> After I looked things over, I stood up and said to the nobles, the officials, and the rest of the people, "Don't be afraid of them. Remember the Lord, who is great and awesome, and fight for your families, your sons and your daughters, your wives and your homes." (Neh. 4:14 NIV)

The speech on that day was short and simple but it was very profound and he challenged them with three great commands— "Don't be afraid of them"; "Remember the Lord"; and "Fight for your families." The leader must know how to bring calm to people in times of crisis but he must also be willing to inspire them to fight for a cause.

10
COLLABORATING FOR A CAUSE

The success of a project is often dependent on the people who work on the project as there are parts of the project that are assigned to individuals and there are other parts where they are expected to work together with other team members. The different segments are then combined and the pieces come together to complete the project. Unfortunately, there are some people who work outside of their assignments and do not put in enough effort, resulting in gaps and incomplete segments. This requires reworking that will cause the project time to be extended and the cost to go up.

There is another problem where some people feel that the tasks they are assigned, is beneath their qualification or their desired role so they constantly grumble, complain or do not do what is asked of them. Feuding and fussing can hinder the work of the mission.

There is a different scenario with the workers who built the wall. The priests worked alongside craftsmen, city officials worked with temple servants, merchants, goldsmiths and perfume makers were all building together. Some of the sections were built by whole families working in unison.

The key to the wall being rebuilt and the mission completed was that the people worked with all their heart. This collaboration and cooperation were necessary because the working conditions were going to get harder.

While the people were busy building the wall, the enemies of progress were busy plotting and planning ways to stop the project. They continued mocking and ridiculing the building program but Nehemiah and his people were focused and kept right on building.

Because the threats of the enemy were real, Nehemiah and his leadership had to go into fight mode and they set up a shift system where some of the people worked, while the others stood guard. They were also equipped with their tools in one hand and a weapon in the other and this was the ultimate strategy of offense and defense. They setup lookouts on the walls with trumpets that would alert the people at the first sign of an attack and they were mission ready because they were in harmony and had a common cause.

In many organizations today, members are fighting each other when they should be united and taking aim at the real enemy. There is a misconception as to who the real enemy is and there is no strategy for them to join forces together against the opposition. Many Christians perceive their brothers and sisters to be the opposition because they don't think like them and agree on various issues. A difference in outlook or opinion is cause for a serious fight and you could possibly be hurt or killed with a spiritual sword.

The builders of the Jerusalem wall were clear about the task at hand, the threat level, what was at stake, and they were ready to face the risks head on. They understood that the strategy had to consist of attacking and defending and even though Nehemiah was not a trained war planner, he established a battle plan that included being equipped and prepared to fight. They were also ready to stand up and protect the wall that was being built, so they positioned guards by night and workers by day to help ensure that there was no damage to the wall or danger to the workers.

There are some important lessons that we can learn from Scripture about working together as a body of believers and leaders must never encourage cliques or factions in the mission as it will divide and bring disunity to the body. We must work together as one under the lordship of Jesus Christ and care for each other.

The Bible reminds us that there is strength in numbers and we must work with each other

> Two are better than one, because they have a good return for their labor If either of them falls down, one can help the other up. But pity anyone who falls and has no one to help them up. Also, if two lie down together, they will keep warm. But how can one keep warm alone?

> Though one may be overpowered, two can defend themselves. A cord of three strands is not quickly broken. (Eccles. 4:9–12 NIV)

We can make each other better when we collaborate and the goal should always be to help the other person improve

> As iron sharpens iron, so one person sharpens another (Prov. 27:17 NIV).

The key to productivity is to encourage and motivate each other

> And let us consider how we may spur one another on toward love and good deeds, not giving up meeting together, as some are in the habit of doing, but encouraging one another, and all the more as you see the Day approaching. (Heb. 10:24–25 NIV)

There are many references in the Bible to the Church as a body because it is joined as one in Christ and should function the way our bodies function in harmony and complementing each part

> Just as a body, though one, has many parts, but all its many parts form one body, so it is with Christ. For we were all baptized by one Spirit so as to form one body, whether Jews or Gentiles, slave

or free, and we were all given the one Spirit to drink. Even so the body is not made up of one part but of many.

Now if the foot should say, "Because I am not a hand, I do not belong to the body," it would not for that reason stop being part of the body. And if the ear should say, "Because I am not an eye, I do not belong to the body," it would not for that reason stop being part of the body. If the whole body were an eye, where would the sense of hearing be? If the whole body were an ear, where would the sense of smell be? But in fact, God has placed the parts in the body, every one of them, just as he wanted them to be. If they were all one part, where would the body be? As it is, there are many parts, but one body. The eye cannot say to the hand, "I don't need you!" And the head cannot say to the feet, "I don't need you!" On the contrary, those parts of the body that seem to be weaker are indispensable, and the parts that we think are less honorable we treat with special honor. And the parts that are unpresentable are treated with special modesty, while our presentable parts need no special treatment. But God has put the body together, giving greater honor to the parts that lacked it, so that there should be no division in the body, but that its parts should have equal concern for each other. If one part suffers, every part suffers with it; if one part is honored, every part rejoices with it.

Now you are the body of Christ, and each one of you is a part of it. (1 Cor. 12:12–27 NIV)

We may not have the same viewpoint or see things in the same way, but we can walk together in unity and we should make a conscious effort to do it

Do two walk together unless they have agreed to do so? (Amos 3:3 NIV)

11
COMPLETING THE MISSION

The day of the project launch and the day of completion, are the two days a project leader looks forward to, as this signifies the beginning and the end and even though they may be months or years apart, they are milestones that represent the body of work that has been done.

Nehemiah was looking forward to the completion of the project and recorded the days in the book. "So, the wall was completed on the twenty-fifth of Elul, in fifty-two days (Neh. 6:15 NIV)." This was remarkable that a whole city wall was built in that time frame without power tools, heavy equipment or machinery. They may not have had these things but they had all they needed to make it happen and when the right combination is in place, the work will be completed and the mission will be accomplished.

There are some important lessons you need to learn from this project and apply them in your various areas of leadership as they will be helpful for your work and ministry.

The first lesson is that the people were committed to the work and we see that in this verse, "So we rebuilt the wall till all of it reached half its height, for the people worked with all their heart (Neh. 4:6 NIV)." The King James Version gives a different rendering of the text, "the people had a mind to work." All of it describes people who bought in to the vision and put out all their effort to see that the work was done even when they faced threats and their lives were at risk from their enemies.

They worked together as one and was united in their purpose. Even though they worked in various sections of the wall, they met and combined the sections together so that it was strong and secure. People working in harmony and committed to a cause are unbeatable and unbreakable and will always win because the power of numbers and the power of unity is stronger than machines or tools.

The second lesson is that leaders must be fearless, insightful and know how to motivate people to get the job done. Nehemiah was that kind of leader and we see that from this account in the book

> After I looked things over, I stood up and said to the nobles, the officials and the rest of the people, "Don't be afraid of them. Remember the Lord, who is great and awesome, and fight for your families, your sons and your daughters, your wives and your homes. When our enemies heard that we were aware of

their plot and that God had frustrated it, we all returned to the wall, each to our own work.

From that day on, half of my men did the work, while the other half were equipped with spears, shields, bows, and armor. The officers posted themselves behind all the people of Judah who were building the wall. Those who carried materials did their work with one hand and held a weapon in the other, and each of the builders wore his sword at his side as he worked. But the man who sounded the trumpet stayed with me.

Then I said to the nobles, the officials and the rest of the people, "The work is extensive and spread out, and we are widely separated from each other along the wall. Wherever you hear the sound of the trumpet, join us there. Our God will fight for us!" So, we continued the work with half the men holding spears, from the first light of dawn till the stars came out. At that time, I also said to the people, "Have every man and his helper stay inside Jerusalem at night, so they can serve us as guards by night and as workers by day. (Neh. 4:14–22 NIV)

The project was well on the way and the enemies were threatening to not only stop the building project but kill the people. Nehemiah had a double responsibility to ensure that the project continued and that the people were protected and secure. He came up with a strategy to ensure that he took care of both tasks.

He encouraged the people, showed them that he cared and had a plan for their safety and protection. He also had to keep them working, even while they were preparing for battle.

The third reason for their success was that God helped them and Nehemiah acknowledged this - "When all our enemies heard about this, all the surrounding nations were afraid and lost their self-confidence, because they realized that this work had been done with the help of our God (Neh. 6:16 NIV)." He knew that even with all the planning and strategy, they still needed to call on the Lord and seek His help and protection. The work was great and there was a lot to be done but they were also under a threat from the enemy. The wise leader will always go to God with the problems that they face and give Him credit for the success of their work. When others see the hand of God in the work of your ministry, it will bring fear to them for they will see and know that God is on your side, fighting for you and doing a good work on your behalf. However, it is very important that we let others know it is all of God and that we publicly give Him the praise and glory for everything that He does.

The work was completed in record time and it was far beyond their expectations and the wishes of their enemies. No power or force can hinder people who are united and dedicated to the service of God and have a love for His work. They will be successful when they are led by men and women of God who know how to pray and intercede with God, listen to His voice and be willing to carry out His work with courage and humility.

Paul outlined to Timothy what a leader should be like and gave him a good description of what a leader should do. This is the kind of leader that gets the job done and completes the mission:

> In the presence of God and of Christ Jesus, who will judge the living and the dead, and in view of His appearing and His kingdom, I give you this charge: Preach the word; be prepared in season and out of season; correct, rebuke and encourage with great patience and careful instruction. For the time will come when people will not put up with sound doctrine. Instead, to suit their own desires, they will gather around them a great number of teachers to say what their itching ears want to hear.
>
> They will turn their ears away from the truth and turn aside to myths. But you, keep your head in all situations, endure hardship, do the work of an evangelist, discharge all the duties of your ministry. (2 Tim. 4:1–5 NIV)

PART 2: VISION

12
A MISSIONARY IS
A VISIONARY

A person who is committed to a mission already has been given a glimpse of the future and understands the possibilities. They have a vision of what could be done and they are excited and motivated to pursue the mission. Often, their family and friends do not see the same possibilities and do not share the vision, so they are in a lonely place with their lofty dreams and ideas.

Visions are not always shared by people in your inner circle and although it's in your heart and mind you cannot discuss it or let anyone else know about where you are heading.

While Nehemiah was in the king's service as the cup-bearer, he had this vision to return to Jerusalem to build the wall. Had he shared his vision with another servant in the palace, they would think he was crazy to give up his dream job to go to work amongst the rubble of the broken-down wall surrounded by misery, despair, and desolation. They would question his skill set for such a mission and ask where he would get the resources to undertake such a major project.

The whispering would go on throughout the palace that Nehemiah was leaving his position to go on a mission to build a wall in Jerusalem. The word would eventually get to the king and he would end up not having a position or a mission.

My word of caution is that you cannot share your vision with everyone. I learned this the hard way as I have shared my visions with people who I felt were spiritual and caring. I asked them for prayer, only to hear later from other sources that I was getting into things I had no business with and that I felt I was a superhero trying to solve all the problems of the world. The life of a visionary is a lonely life, but If you're going to be a missionary, you must be a visionary who is willing to carry the burden alone.

Jesus tried to share with His disciples what His mission here was all about and they completely misunderstood Him. Some thought He had come to establish political power and rule here on earth. This was so rooted in their minds that the mother of two of the disciples came to lobby for key positions for her sons when He came to power. She specified that she would like to have one seated on the right hand and the other on the left hand in His cabinet meetings. He was talking about a heavenly kingdom but they could not visualize that because they had an earthly mindset. They had this vision of ruling the kingdoms of the earth and they did not get the true meaning of what Jesus was talking about when He told them very plainly that His kingdom was not of this earth.

He further shared with them how it would all end. He told them He would die on a cross and suffer as a sacrifice for the sins of the world and that He would be buried and on the third day rise again. His inner circle could not perceive it and one of his key disciples lashed out and rebuked Him for even mentioning such a thing. They did not see it that way, therefore, they were not going to receive it or believe it because they had a different vision of who He was and His purpose here on earth.

Visions are not only burdensome as you must carry its weight by yourself, but they can be troublesome and can cause trouble for you. Visionaries are not always welcomed and the more you talk about your vision and the things you are going to do, the more your haters and detractors will be angry. They will seek ways to not only to shut down your project but to kill you and all who are associated with it. Nehemiah discovered that as he started out on his project and he learned very early that the people who don't like your vision, do not want to see it fulfilled. The reason is, that you're on a positive mission to build and they're on a negative mission to tear down.

Nehemiah traveled to Jerusalem with letters of recommendation and verification from the king as well as an entourage of attendants and guards. However, when he went to scope out the project, he went by night and he went by himself. He did not want anyone in his entourage to know where he was going or what he was doing so he waited until night when they had gone to sleep and explored the city wall.

The people who had traveled with him knew the prestigious office he held in the palace as the king's cup-bearer and they held him in high regard. Here he was now, in a desolate, broken-down place with no sign of hope or possibilities. Had he taken them with him on his site survey, he would not be able to convince them that this was a viable project and that the wall could be built and the city put back together. They would brand him as a person who was overzealous and trying to do too much. They might also go as far as to say that he was wasting the king's resources by bringing them along to accompany him there and acquiring the materials the king had given him for a project that was not attainable.

Do not try to get pessimists to see your vision as they only see what's wrong and they will not be able to see what's possible. This is one of the reasons why people do not want to be missionaries because a missionary is a visionary and they both live in another world. It is a place where all things are possible, where old thing becomes new and the light shines in and overcomes the darkness. A vision comes only to those who are ready to believe and receive. It is not for those with blinded eyes and hardened hearts.

13
SEEING TOMORROW TODAY

We talk a lot about today and tomorrow and we are constantly reminded to live in the moment for all we have is today because yesterday is gone and tomorrow may never come. We are also encouraged to live today as if it's our last as there are no guarantees of tomorrow.

These are some good thoughts and it would do you good to live by them. However, while there is no guarantee that you will be alive tomorrow, you must still believe that tomorrow is possible. If it is possible, we would like it to be a good tomorrow or even a better tomorrow.

You must believe that as bad as today is, tomorrow can be the time for things to turn around and be a better day. It gives hope for change and transformation and allows you to think that where you are lacking today, you can make up for it tomorrow. The mistakes that you make today can be corrected tomorrow. You may be sick today but healed tomorrow, broke today but get some money tomorrow, lose a relationship but can find someone else tomorrow. This is what tomorrow means because it signifies renewal, revival, and hope.

Moses led the people through the wilderness but because of his disobedience, he was not allowed to lead them into the promised land. God had appointed Joshua as the chosen leader to take them there. However, God took him up to the mountain and showed him the land afar off and he could see the lush green fields, the hills, the valleys, the rivers, and lakes. He saw the possibilities of what it would be like to live there, what could be done and how it would be. He knew he would not get there because God had already told him but that did not stop him from visualizing it. Before Joshua and the people entered the land in person, Moses already saw what it looked like.

Visionaries are like Moses and they are on the hill looking out into the land afar off. It is a place they have not reached and may not get there, but they can see it. While the people are on the ground, visionaries have an aerial view and this gives them insight into what it could be like.

While we are living today, we are already peering past the failures, the disappointments, the ridicule, and setbacks. We do not have a full understanding, but we can see the layout and can see the shape of tomorrow, we don't have all the facts or the data but we know it will happen. We got a vision and now we know it is not just something we hoped for but it is real, and tomorrow we will get there.

That's what it was like for Nehemiah. Hanani, and the men who brought him the news had all the information about what was happening for they had been there and seen the desolation and despair. This was the reality of the situation and the men gave Nehemiah a factual and honest report. He knew it was a true account and it was that truth that moved him to pray a prayer of repentance and cry out to God for forgiveness on behalf of his people.

However, despite the present reality, he saw a tomorrow where the walls that were crumbled, the gates that had fallen and the city that was desolate being rebuilt, restored and made whole again. He saw that which was dead today being made alive tomorrow.

Visionaries see dead churches, dead marriages, dead cities and hopeless people all around them today. They also know that the power of the risen Lord can bring new life into those churches, marriages, cities, people and cause them to live again. Tomorrow is all about being dead today but alive tomorrow. Tomorrow says to the visionary, I may be down today but once the clock goes past midnight and a new day breaks, it brings hope and a bright future. May we see tomorrow today for a brighter day is coming . . . tomorrow.

14

THE STRENGTH OF A VISION

V isions arise out of feelings of despair, disappointment, and discouragement and they come at a time when we are at our lowest and experiencing the pain of loss and deprivation.

Ancient cities depended on walls for protection against intruders, wild animals and other nations that were planning to invade and overtake them. The wall was important for the nation's peace and prosperity. The gates which were a part of the city wall also played an important role in the city's trade and commerce. Important meetings and matters of government were held at the city gates. If the walls were broken down and the city gates were destroyed, this meant that the entire nation was greatly affected and there was a lot at stake. That was the very reason the invading army had burnt down the wall and broken the gates. It was a strategy to cripple the city.

When Nehemiah got news about the city walls, he could connect it right away and he understood the significance. The visionary must be able to connect the dots and be able to understand the meaning of the times we live in. That is what caused the men of the tribe of Issachar to stand out for they understood the times and knew what Israel should do (1 Chron. 12:32 NIV).

In our day, there is no shortage of outlets online and on air that brings us an abundance of negativity. It is not that what they are reporting is not factual and did not happen but it is the way it is highlighted, repeated and continually talked about. Do you wonder why there is a rise in depression, mental illness and other ailments? It is because we are constantly bombarded with stories about all that's wrong in the world and it begins to weigh heavily on us. There are pundits and commentators on air that you will never get a good news story from them because their job is to be bearers of news about broken walls and burned gates.

Once Nehemiah got to the city and personally observed the ruins and the desolation, he stood up against the backdrop of the broken wall like the news reporters do in our day. However, he did not just talk about it but rather used it as an opportunity to challenge them to rebuild the wall and get the city back to life again. This message resonated with the people and they all responded to the message and declared in unison, "let us start rebuilding!" (Nehemiah 2:18 NIV)

They grasped the vision and realized that something could be done and what this man was saying was possible and achievable. In his speech to them, he no doubt shared his own grief and conviction when he first heard the story. However, he further went on to share about what God had placed on his heart and his journey from being a cupbearer in the king's palace to being a missionary. He was now ready to participate and help lead the rebuilding effort.

This message of hope and renewal must be proclaimed from the many churches in our nation and the vision should also be echoed from city halls and Congress. It will not only be done by a speech or a talk but by people who understand the seriousness of the times and are willing to do something about it.

This is a tremendous time of opportunity for the visionaries to come forth and declare the strength of a vision and share it with all who would listen. As visionaries, this is the message you must bring:

Understand that even though evil is present and there are acts of violence in your cities, Jesus is offering real change and transformation and new life is possible in Him and through Him. The reality is that every sinner can be changed.

Recognize that there are people who struggle with personal problems and you should deal with them in different ways. Understand that each person is loved by God and He cares about their struggles and difficulties and they have a unique potential to be transformed.

Acknowledge that personal strengths are displayed in various ways and the skills and talents of each person deserve to be identified, engaged, and nurtured. This was evident in the volunteers that came to build with Nehemiah

Diligently try to find new ways to enhance your community's lifestyles. Help technically challenged citizens to get up to speed with the new and changing realities of the present times and see your people advance together.

Invest your time, money and talent in the development of your communities.

Assert that for the community to be successful, all the people must succeed and you would do all that's possible for that to be realized.

Seek to prioritize the well-being of your members and the achievement of all your people. This must rise above divisive ideological goals and objectives.

Endeavor to develop and build a caring community that would encourage openness, love, and respect and work together for growth and prosperity.

Vision is asking you to deny yourself, make sacrifices, be willing to go beyond and above yourself and do all that is necessary to make the mission a reality.

Vision demands that you would be willing to become not only hearers of the word but doers of the word and faithfully devote yourself to do that which the Lord has called you to do so that you can experience the strength of a vision.

15

THE SIZE OF A VISION

A vision starts out small and increases in size as it becomes clearer. It begins with a desire to do something and at the time, it is just an idea that develops in your mind. Eventually, it captures your heart and occupies your spirit in a way that demands your attention and you can no longer be passive.

Visions have the capacity to grow into what I refer to as "God sized proportions." When God gives you a vision, it is larger than anything that you can comprehend and it ascends above your reach. It becomes very demanding and causes you to stretch further than your capabilities. As a human, you are limited in your ability to perceive or understand the future. However, when God places a vision in you, it is always about the future and therefore, since He is the God who knows the future, you must trust Him for the outcome of the vision.

Since it is God who determines the size of the vision, you must seek to expand your mind and by His Spirit, be always ready to see what He has in mind for you and the vision He is calling you to. Whenever He sends the vision, He also gives the enabling to fulfill it. He promises in the book of Joel, "I will pour out my Spirit on all people. Your sons and daughters will prophesy, your old men will dream dreams, your young men will see visions (Joel 2:28 NIV)."

The blessings you are experiencing today are what the people who have gone before dreamt about. They did not have a full understanding or real picture of what it would look like, but it was on their mind and in their heart and they longed for it and prayed for it. In the same way, God is pouring out His Spirit on this generation and the young people are receiving a fresh vision and a powerful revelation from God. He is using their skills and abilities to do a new thing in this new age.

In the book of John chapter 19, the disciples were gathered together in a locked room because they were afraid of the Jewish leaders and the possibility of persecution. They were just a few believers who had no idea of what was going to happen and where they were going. Their master had been crucified and they were not sure if this message that He had been preaching could continue. While they were in this state of fear, uncertainty, and doubt, Jesus appeared to them. He displayed His nail-scarred hands, and He calmed their fears by giving them His peace. He told them that He was going to send them out into the world as His Father had sent Him. He then breathed on them and poured out His Spirit on them. In that moment, they were transformed from fearful and timid men to powerful, Spirit-led disciples who flooded their world with the life-changing message of Jesus. They went everywhere spreading the gospel message not only in the synagogues but also in the towns and villages. They traveled thousands of miles on donkeys and by foot to preach to all who would hear and many received the word and believed and the church grew.

The 21st-century Church is now once again locked into rooms and buildings and we have built fantastic structures where we gather for worship. I'm not criticizing or diminishing the building programs of any church or ministry because I have been part of helping to build some of these structures and do worship in a large facility. However, the ministries of the future and the churches of tomorrow will no longer be housed in a building between four walls. The Holy Spirit has now come as He did with the early church and He has empowered us and given us a new challenge to go forth into the world with the message of Christ. In our times, the vision has been enlarged, and we have a greater population than when they started out. Our world has expanded so much more geographically, politically and economically and we are now dealing with different issues and new opportunities.

Although the spirit of the vision is the same and message of the early church is the same, the ministries of the future and the church of the future have changed dynamically. In the new reality, people are no longer coming into buildings to participate in a worship experience, they have gone elsewhere, and to them, the Church is no longer relevant.

If they have abandoned the Church and no longer attend services, then, where are they? What are they doing and why are they there? These are the important questions that not only ministry leaders must ask, but the entire body of believers must begin to assess what is happening and how effective are we in our impact.

From our evaluations and observations, the people who were once in the church pews and pulpits were now on the Internet. They are trying to get from social media what they once got from the Church—love, relationships, fulfillment, affirmation, peace and contentment and something to believe in. I'm not going to argue whether the Church is no longer offering these things or the people have just gone off to a new and different fountain to try to find satisfaction for their thirst for God. However, I will strongly declare that we need to go out and meet them where they are. Instead of spending enormous resources in trying to get them to come back into the four walls, let us expand our visions and try to reach them where they are.

16
THE STORY OF
THE VISION

Twenty-five years ago, I was not able to connect to the Internet or check my email from a smartphone. When I had my devotional time, or needed to check a portion of Scripture, I reached for my big, thick leather-covered Bible to read what I wanted. It was thick because it had a full concordance, notes, Scripture references, maps of the apostle's missionary journeys and maps of the cities mentioned in the Scriptures. I can now access all of that on my cell phone and not only read it but make notes, email it or message it to my brothers from my Bible study and if I get really blessed by what I read and I want the world to know, I send out a tweet. When it's time for Scripture reading at church, there are an increasing number of cell phones and tablets that are displayed and people are following the Scripture reading from their devices. There is also a new change in the pulpit and many of the sermons are now delivered from a tablet. Welcome to the 21st century and the digital age! We are experiencing a new and different world that has rapidly changed by technology and it is getting more advanced with the introduction of new applications and innovations.

We are also in the new missionary age and living in a different time to when the apostles traveled across their world on donkeys and on foot. The early missionaries of our time traveled by ships, bus and trains. We can now get up at mornings, and before we get out of bed, write a blog, upload it and get it to a worldwide audience in less than thirty minutes.

The mission field has also changed and we are now able to reach people that we have never seen or known. We can minister to people that live in places we have never been and people that would not accept our invitation to church or Bible study. However, they are right there when we log on and they are open to chat, share stories, pictures and ideas. There are many people on social media full time who always have their pages open and constantly messaging and posting even while they are at work.

Jesus understood that this would happen when He sent out the seventy-two mission workers and He had this generation in mind as well. Here's what He said to the workers as He was commissioning them. He told them, "The harvest is plentiful, but the workers are few. Ask the Lord of the harvest, therefore, to send out workers into His harvest field. Go, I am sending you out like lambs among wolves (Luke 10:2,3 NIV)." He described it as an abundant harvest that was ready for reaping but there was a limited number of workers available for the task. That seems to be a true description of our times. There are a great number of preachers, evangelists, prophets, apostles, priests, pastors, and ministers but very few online missionaries who are reaching people where they are. Jesus said that there was a great harvest field out there consisting of people hungry and thirsty for God. However, they could not find Him who is the bread of life and the living water because the people who had the bread and water, were at their designated place of gathering, distributing and giving it to people who are already filled. They have had appetizers, a full entree with dessert and they keep coming every Sunday and Wednesday for more. The ones who are filled should be getting out and sharing it with people who need help, hope, love, and peace.

The mission field has changed and the methods are new and innovative but we must preach the same message that the early disciples preached of Jesus's love for people. His ability to touch, heal and deliver and the final results of judgment for those who disobey His call to repentance. This message is vital to the salvation of those who are lost and perishing. Some people only tell it in an established place, at a regular time, and it is told only by people who are assigned to tell it. This message is more critical than any vaccine or medicine that are important for the saving of lives because it's not only about the life we now live but it is about eternity and the life hereafter. Jesus saw it as important because in the same text in Luke 10, He gave them instructions about where they were to go and the methods they were to utilize to get out the message. He also gave them a specific message that they were to tell those who would listen. He told them, "Heal the sick who are there and tell them, the kingdom of God has come near to you (Luke 10:9

NIV)." This message was for the people who were out-side of the kingdom of God and He was trying to get them into His Kingdom. There is a different scenario in the fellowship of believers today and I'm not just criticizing or attacking any specific church or ministry but this is for the whole body. The question is, why are you preaching salvation to people who are already in the kingdom? You give the same messages over and over to the believers and ignore the people who are not in the kingdom.

If you were to use Jesus's message of the harvest field as an example, the question then would be to all. Why do you keep harvesting a field where the grapes have already been picked and ignore the field where the fruit is hanging to the ground and need harvesting? Perhaps, that is what He was referring to when He said the laborers are few. They may be avail-able, but they are busy in the field where the harvest has already taken place and do not see the hanging fruit over in the next field. The vision story then is that we see the fields that are ready to harvest. However, let us not just ask the Lord to send workers to reap the harvest but that we are the workers who will get in the fields and start harvesting. You don't have to look too far or go to some foreign field to see that the harvest is abundant for it is right on your computer or smart-phone screen every day and it is all around you. The problem is that we've been thinking all along that it is only when they come through the doors of the church and come to the altar in response to a sermon that the harvest is being reaped. The key to Jesus's call to the seventy-two was when He asked them to pray that

God would send out workers and He told them that He was also sending them out like lambs among wolves.

The emphasis needs to be changed from bringing people in to a service to sending out workers to serve. When that happens, the vision of the harvest will increase and you will see fields that are ripe and ready to harvest. You must get to the real task of healing the community and preaching the message of the Kingdom.

17
VISION PURPOSE

Throughout Scripture, God's purpose for giving visions to people was to send messages to them about what He was going to do in the future. He sent a message in a vision to Pharaoh about what was going to happen in Egypt. He was troubled by it but Joseph gave him the interpretation of the vision and it came to pass just as he said. Nebuchadnezzar had a similar vision regarding his future in Babylon and God sent Daniel to give him the meaning of the vision which also came to pass.

God spoke to Ananias in a vision concerning Saul of Tarsus at the time of his conversion and told him where Saul was and his need for someone to minister to him. Later, Saul whose name was changed to Paul, and who also became an apostle, saw in a vision a man from Macedonia asking him to come over and help them. Paul went there and preached the gospel to them.

A vision is not just a dream that you have at night after a late supper. It is something that God reveals to you and places in your heart. It may not be clear initially, but He will show you His purpose for the vision and how He wants you to fulfill it.

Individuals and organizations put together vision statements as a guide to help them follow the vision of how they would like to see things looking in the future. A vision statement is different to a mission statement as the vision statement conveys a picture of what the individual or organization will be in the future and it outlines the best possible state as an outcome.

Nehemiah's vision statement could have been "to see the city restored and the nation reformed after the walls have been rebuilt." This was reflected in his prayer as he prayed to God:

> Remember the instruction you gave your servant Moses, saying, "If you are unfaithful, I will scatter you among the nations, but if you return to me and obey my commands, then even if your exiled people are at the farthest horizon, I will gather them from there and bring them to the place I have chosen as a dwelling for my Name. (Neh. 1:8, 9 NIV)

The broken wall, burnt gates, and destroyed city resulted in the people being scattered and the nation in disarray. However, as the wall and the city gates were rebuilt, the city would provide safety and security for the residents and their lives would be restored to the normal state. It troubled Nehemiah greatly that the people were scattered, temple worship had ceased and there was no word from the Lord. As a result, the people had departed from the laws and commandments of God and everything was in chaos and confusion so he made it his mission to rebuild the wall. The real purpose was not to just build a wall and return home but rather, to see the city restored and the people reformed, revived, changed, and transformed.

When you build, it should not be about the building, its size and beauty. It is about its purpose as a place for gathering to worship. The building is for people to be instructed in God's word and for training and service. After the building is completed, the real work of preaching, teaching, fellowship, and discipleship must take place. The purpose is to have a thriving congregation that will reach out into the surrounding community and make a difference by bringing people into Christ's kingdom.

The wall was built on time and budget because the people were enthusiastic to work despite the opposition and threats from the enemy. They did whatever was necessary to complete the building of the wall. However, because the project was completed, it did not mean that the work was done. It was just getting started as the vision purpose still had to be fulfilled and there was a long road ahead.

It is easy to get people to buy into the mission when it is something tangible that they can see and touch. However, it is a different thing to convey a vision that God gives to the leader who is the visionary. It is in his heart and mind and transferred to paper in the form of a vision purpose statement. Getting people to understand it, buy into it and believe it, is difficult. The leader must now pray and depend on God to make this vision clear to the people as God is the one who causes people to see His purpose for their lives.

There is a great story that demonstrates this in the Old Testament where the king of Aram was upset with Elisha because he was giving intelligence reports to the king of Israel that allowed him to escape his attacks. The king of Aram decided to capture Elisha and sent his men with horses and chariots to surround the city where he was. Elisha's servant got up early the next morning and saw the strong force that surrounded the city and he was terrified and cried out to his master in panic and despair. Elisha gave him a great response

> "Don't be afraid," the prophet answered. "Those who are with us are more than those who are with them." And Elisha prayed, "Open his eyes, Lord, so that he may see." Then the Lord opened the servant's eyes, and he looked and saw the hills full of horses and chariots of fire all around Elisha. (2 Kings 6:16–17 NIV)

Every leader should pray for their followers the same prayer Elisha prayed for his servant. They must pray that the Lord would open their eyes that they could see that God is with them and will work on their behalf even as they are surrounded by obstacles and people that would try to hinder them. The groups and the congregations need to see and understand what God is going to do in the future and what He has revealed to you as the leader. However, you must pray for their eyes to be opened so that they get a view of the future of the ministry. If they don't get it, they will be like Elisha's servant, who was scared and confused. The message should be strong and clear that they need not be afraid because God has a purpose for the vision and the future is in His hands.

Below are some great vision verses which that will help you to see the purpose of God.

> Where there is no vision, the people perish: but he that keepeth the law, happy is he. (Prov. 29:18 KJV)

> For the vision is yet for an appointed time, but at the end it shall speak, and not lie: though it tarry, wait for it; because it will surely come, it will not tarry. (Hab. 2:3 KJV)

> Once you spoke in a vision, to your faithful people you said: "I have bestowed strength on a warrior; I have raised up a young man from among the people." (Ps. 89:19 NIV)

> What we have received is not the spirit of the world, but the Spirit who is from God, so that we may understand what God has freely given us.

> This is what we speak, not in words taught us by human wisdom but in words

taught by the Spirit, explaining spiritual realities with Spirit-taught words.

The person without the Spirit does not accept the things that come from the Spirit of God but considers them foolishness, and cannot understand them because they are discerned only through the Spirit.

The person with the Spirit makes judgments about all things, but such a person is not subject to merely human judgments. (1 Cor. 2:12–15 NIV)

I keep asking that the God of our Lord Jesus Christ, the glorious Father, may give you the Spirit of wisdom and revelation, so that you may know Him better.

I pray that the eyes of your heart may be enlightened in order that you may know the hope to which He has called you, the riches of His glorious inheritance in His holy people. (Eph. 1:17–18 NIV)

For God does speak, now one way, now another, though no one perceives it. (Job 33:14 NIV)

One night the Lord spoke to Paul in a vision: "Do not be afraid; keep

on speaking, do not be silent."
(Acts 18:9 NIV)

Meanwhile, the people were waiting
for Zechariah and wondering why he
stayed so long in the temple. When he
came out, he could not speak to them.
They realized he had seen a vision in
the temple, for he kept making signs
to them but remained unable to speak.
When his time of service was completed,
he returned home. (Luke 1:21–23 NIV)

The boy Samuel ministered before the
Lord under Eli. In those days, the word
of the Lord was rare; there were not
many visions. (1 Sam. 3:1 NIV)

And afterward, I will pour out my Spirit
on all people. Your sons and daughters will prophesy, your old men will
dream dreams, your young men will see
visions. (Joel 2:28 NIV)

18
VISION PERSPECTIVE

V isions are personal, but how we view them, relate to them and react to them are important. They can have a great impact not only on us but on the lives of other people and greatly influence their outlook.

We see in the book of Numbers chapter 13 When the children of Israel were on their way to the Promised Land, God approached Moses and told him to send some men on an exploration mission to Canaan to check out the land. Moses selected a representative from each of the tribes and gave them specific instructions for the mission. They were to go to the southern area of Canaan, specifically in the hill country, and see what the land was like. They were checking to see if it was a fortified city with walls. They were also to inspect the soil to see whether it was fertile and what kind of trees were growing there. He also told them to bring back some samples of the fruit. The study was to include the kind of people that lived in the land, the population, their strengths, weaknesses, and how they lived.

This was a complete demographics study that had to be done and they were gone for forty days as it was a vast land area that had to be covered and it required them to collect a lot of information. When they returned, they were expected to submit a complete report of their findings to Moses and the people. The report was to be verbal and visual. They were instructed to bring back evidence of what was going on in the land as this would enable them to do a thorough analysis and determine a strategy for entering it.

They came back to the whole Israelite community and presented their reports. Ten of the twelve men who had gone on the mission gave their account of the land and showed the fruit they had brought back with them. They reported that the land was flowing with milk and honey, the soil was fertile, and there was good fruit. However, the people who lived there were powerful, the cities were fortified and very large. There were people dwelling there who they had encountered before in fierce battle during their travels through the desert land, and those people were stronger and bigger than them. To make their point, they told the gathering that compared to the men of the city, they seemed like grasshoppers. (Numbers 13:32-33 NIV) They summarized their report by recommending that it would not be a good idea to attack the people of the land since they were stronger and the Israelites would not be able to defeat them. It was a negative report and it caused the people to be discouraged and disheartened. They also concluded that according to the findings in this report, it could not be done.

There were two men, Caleb and Joshua, who had gone on the same mission, for the same length of time and saw the same things but their report was completely different. They stood up and calmed the people at the gathering. They agreed that powerful people were living there who were bigger and stronger and there were things that might be negative. However, their conclusion was that they should go up and take possession of the land for they had the ability and strength to overcome the giants and take the land.

How is it that in their survey, they saw the same things but in their analysis, they saw things differently? It is about vision perspective and how you see what is before you, your understanding of the situation and the angle from which you view it.

Ten people came back saying we are not able but two came back saying, we are well able. The majority voices were loud and they convinced the people that this was the case and they believed the negative report that caused them to panic and despair. It is at this moment that visionaries must stand up and declare to their people that they must not be afraid of what is before them for they have the strength and the power to overcome and take possession of their destiny.

Nehemiah had a positive perspective of the city that was in ruins and he had the vision to rebuild the wall that was broken. He went to the people and challenged them to become part of the movement that would bring transformation to the city and they believed his message, bought into his vision and decided to build the wall.

The city officials who were against the mission came up with some strong criticism of the project and mocked the work that they were doing.

> When Sanballat heard that we were rebuilding the wall, he became angry and was greatly incensed. He ridiculed the Jews, and in the presence of his associates and the army of Samaria, he said, "What are those feeble Jews doing? Will they restore their wall? Will they offer sacrifices? Will they finish in a day? Can they bring the stones back to life from those heaps of rubble, burned as they are?" Tobiah the Ammonite, who was at his side, said, "What they are building, even a fox climbing up on it would break down their wall of stones!" (Neh. 4:1–3 NIV)

Nehemiah's response to their mean comments was outstanding and a great lesson for leaders when they are under attack and facing unjustified criticism. He turned to God, asking Him to respond and retaliate.

> Hear us, our God, for we are despised. Turn their insults back on their own heads. Give them over as plunder in a land of captivity. Do not cover up their guilt or blot out their sins from your sight, for they have thrown insults in the face of the builders. (Neh. 4:4–5 NIV)

He not only turned to God in prayer for the men who were antagonizing them, but he inspired his people, challenged them to work harder, do more, and they got the job done. It is a good thing to let your enemies and their ridicule be the fuel to get the engine of your mission fired up. Instead of allowing the criticism to slow you down, use it to propel you into your destiny. "So, we rebuilt the wall till all of it reached half its height, for the people worked with all their heart" (Neh. 4:6 NIV).

The negative reports from people who are against moving forward are being heard and their argument is that it has been this way for a long time and we cannot do anything about the situation. Like the ten men, they see giants and obstacles and constantly give verbal and visual messages of gloom and doom and all that is not possible.

However, there are people like Caleb, Joshua, and Nehemiah who believe that it can be done. They are progressive in their outlook and positive in their conviction that you must not only believe it but step out and do it.

19
VISION PATHWAYS

There is a story in 2 Kings 7 that is set during a war between Syria and Samaria where the Syrians targeted the city of Samaria. They blocked all means of getting supplies into the city and choked the economy resulting in a food shortage.

The strategy was a means to create uncertainty and instability within the city that would force them to surrender. By applying economic pressure and bringing hardship to the citizens, the citizens in turn would bring pressure to bear on the leadership to surrender.

The city of Samaria was on the brink of chaos and about to collapse as they were facing serious political, economic, and social crisis. It was a very difficult and perplexing situation. The famine was so severe that we see in 2 Kings 6 that there was a case of two women who decided to cook their children and eat them just to survive.

While all of this was happening inside the city, there were four men outside the city gates. They were out of the mainstream society because they had a leprous condition and according to Jewish law, they had to be cast out of the city because they were unclean. During their time at the city gates, people would go in and out of the city and give them handouts of food, money, clothing, and other offerings. Now that the city was under siege and the gates were closed, their source of supply also dried up and there seemed to be no one to help and no way out of this dilemma.

These men understood their plight very well. They knew the situation was grave and they were aware of what they were up against. Their condition was seriously deteriorating and they concluded that death would be the result. They reasoned that if they went into the city they would starve because there was no food there and if they stayed in their present location they would also die. Death seemed to surround them and although it seemed inevitable, they believed there had to be a way out. As they discussed it, someone asked a significant question, "why stay here until we die?" (2 Kings 7:3 NIV). This caused them to come up with a very unlikely proposition that they should go to the camp of the Syrians and ask for assistance and provisions. Reasoning that they were about to die anyhow and the worst thing that could happen is that the Syrians would kill them and put them out of their misery. There was also a possibility that they would have compassion and spare their lives.

Having settled on that option, they set off for the Syrian camp, but it was not a casual walk as they realized that it was a journey that could result in their death or deliverance. They weren't sure, but each step was bringing them nearer to the outcome and it was very unsettling to think that very shortly they could be dead men or be in a better position than their fellow citizens in Samaria. However, it was a risk they were willing to take as all the other choices pointed to death. They realized that risk is associated with progress and to get to the place they wanted to be, they had to be willing to take a chance, step into the world of the unknown, and go against the odds.

These were four weak, leprous men who were unarmed with no fighting techniques, no military plan or strategy and it was impossible to engage the Syrians in battle. However, as the lepers were making their way to the camp something strange happened. The Lord made the lepers' feet sound as though they were chariot wheels. The Syrians thought the Samaritans had hired mercenaries to help fight against them and they fled their camp, leaving behind all their food, clothes, and provisions. When they arrived at the camp and saw it was empty, the lepers helped themselves to the food and filled up, and then proceeded to sort through the silver, gold, and clothing. They picked out the finest pieces and hid them. These men came to the Syrian camp as poor, sick, weak, starved men; now almost instantaneously they were wealthy, well fed, and well clothed, and better times had come for them. There are times when you should take bold initiatives that take the opposition by surprise, as the lepers had. You might not have a lot to fight with but your bold move and strong stand can cause them to be shaken and confused. You make a move and go forward with firm conviction and strong determination and you will be amazed at what will fall before you. That which seemed insurmountable, impossible, unreachable, untouchable, improbable will vanish and disappear and all things will then become possible.

Their new status brought new challenges as there was a desire to fill up to overflowing. They started to overeat, to overindulge, to engage in excessive behavior, to hoard, hide, and have it all to themselves. These were natural human reactions and it seemed to make sense and justify their position. When you dream big, think up ideas, take risks, take on challenges and it all falls into place, why not enjoy the benefits of your endeavors? While they were enjoying their indulgences, something jolted them and someone declared, "what we're doing is not right. This is a day of good news and we are keeping it to ourselves. Let us go at once and report this to the royal palace." (2 Kings 7:9 NIV)

The people of Samaria were starving and the city was on the verge of collapse. They could save the lives of thousands of people and save the city. This was a time of deliverance for all, not just themselves, they were only instruments of help and salvation for their fellow men.

It was news that all Samaria needed to hear, deliverance had come! How could you not share that news? Life was now possible, there was food, and people need not die. To deny the city the opportunity to participate in this good fortune indeed deserves punishment from the One who helped them discover this wealth. They had to realize that they were just the ones who discovered it and it was not theirs. It was to be a means of life and survival for all Samaria, not just four lepers.

When God entrusts you with great wealth, vast knowledge, and extensive opportunities, it is not just for your personal benefit but for the enhancement of your community. The purpose is that it would be a better place because of you having been here. There is nothing more rewarding and fulfilling than to be a part of the transforming process. To watch situations that were negative and potentially fatal, turn around for the better and to see people experience new life.

A vision should cause you to think about what you are doing and where you are going and it should force you to make choices. You get to the place where you admit that your present state is not adequate and what is being done in your community, church, ministry, school, and city is not good enough. You become unwilling to go on doing what you have always done and refuse to be an innocent bystander looking helplessly at all the things that are happening in these places and do nothing about it. It is at that point that you must take a stand and decide that you will not be pulled into a future that will shape you without your goals in mind. You must not tolerate a situation that will not allow you to have a role in what happens to the place where you live, work, play, learn, and worship.

You must then do what is necessary and step away from that which is holding you captive. You must step into a new reality of hope and possibilities to envision a future that would be efficient and effective.

Identify how it could come into being and what the key elements would look like. Once this is in place, you should then task yourself with building a working model that would become the template for the future and the blueprint for a successful outcome. As you travel the vision pathways, you will understand that God has given you the components to build a sustainable future and you must not waste your time on trivial pursuits but recognize that you can be engaged in a meaningful mission that is worth your commitment. You can feel the assurance to a strong set of values about your community and the place where you work and worship.

The gifts and talents that were given to you by God are for His purpose, and you must use them for His honor and glory and build His kingdom here on earth. In the end, it is only the things that you do for Christ will last. The call is for Christians to get involved in the life of the community and begin to organize projects that will bring change and transformation. You must awaken the cities to the life that Jesus brings, and as Christ followers demonstrate to a watching world that you are change agents and these are the questions to consider.

> What are you doing to help your community transform?

> Are you ready for the challenge?

> Where are you now and where would you like to be?

What are the current resources available?

What current skills and knowledge do you have available?

What actions can you undertake?

How can you get people involved?

What can you do?

What would Jesus do?

You must have the determination to keep doing work that has meaning for the community and to maintain integrity while you are doing it. Above all, you must continue giving life to your deepest desire, to serve God and His people and do the things that you are called to do. You must never be afraid to do the things that will contribute to a better life for all.

Nehemiah stepped out of his comfort zone and into an unknown situation and it resulted in a wonderful transformation for the people and the city. You can learn these lessons of trust, obedience, and faith and watch God do His work.

20
VISION PROCESS

A vision does not come all at once and it is not always clear at first. It is like a foggy morning where you get out on the road to start your journey but there are patches of fog across the road that allows you to see just enough to keep going. However, as you proceed, you see the rest and you keep going, trusting what you can see. You know where you are going and have the directions to get there but the road is not clear so you can only see a few feet ahead and it means that you will have to travel at a limited speed.

This can be frustrating at times, especially if you're in a hurry to get to your destination and have a deadline to meet. In this situation, there is not much you can do but go with the flow. The alternative is to accelerate or go at regular speed and risk running into the vehicle ahead of you or swerving off the road and getting into an accident.

On a foggy day, it is highly recommended that all drivers turn on their lights as this will assist with visibility but it also allows you to see the car ahead and be able to see how close you are to it.

Do you see a parallel here with your life's journey? You know exactly where you would like to go and how to get there but once you hit the road and start to travel, the fog comes in your path. You must slow down and drive at a slower speed but this will also affect your estimated time of arrival at your destination. Frustration and anger can result from this situation because in our hectic, fast-paced society we get upset when we have full schedules and packed agendas that have time limits attached and we do not have extra time to spare.

As in the case of driving on the road in your car, the recommendation here is to turn on your lights so you can have extended vision, see what is ahead of you and avoid crashing or swerving off the road. It would be helpful to slow down as well.

What is the light that we turn on in this situation? It is the light of the Word of God which David refers to in Psalms as a lamp unto our feet and a light to our path (Ps. 119:105 KJV). When the light of God is turned on, our spiritual eyes are opened and the vision becomes clearer.

The vision process can be slow at times, as it was for Nehemiah. It was quite some time between the time he got the call to mission and the completion of the mission. Although he had a vision for what he wanted to do, it did not come together all at once and he had to wait for God's timing and follow His lead.

The process took him through various phases and places in his life and he learned several lessons from them:

Dialogue and Discussion Process— His meeting with his brother and the men who came from Jerusalem was a forum for open and frank dialogue. He learned that when you ask hard questions, you must be prepared for hard answers and asking specific questions will result in clear and concise answers.

He also learned that truth telling and an honest assessment of the situation is essential for an understanding of the conditions and when you ask questions out of concern and a caring perspective, it brings a compassionate response

Discovery Process—He learned that inquiry leads to discovery and asking the right questions leads to new possibilities.

It is important to get accurate information from reliable sources.

Discovery of the facts are not always pleasant but it will give insights into the reality of what is taking place.

Ask people who are knowledgeable and involved in the situation.

Direct and honest answers lead to active involvement.

Digging Deep Process—He was moved by the report

He turned to God, the One who could help, in prayer.

His high view of God led him to understand that God sees, hears, and knows everything.

He had a clear picture of the sinful condition of his people and himself.

He saw God as the faithful One who keeps His word and His promises are sure.

He appealed to God to grant mercy to His redeemed people.

Decision Process—By the end of the prayer, Nehemiah knew that it was not enough to pray and believe and he had to do something about the existing condition.

If the situation was going to be fixed, he was going to have to do something.

Direction Process—He asked God to give him success and favor in his venture.

Before he talked to his king, he talked to his God.

He recognized the leading of God and the hand of God in his life.

Destiny Process—Because of his high office and relationship to the king, he was not only able to get approval for his mission but also to get the goods and supplies he needed.

The people believed in his vision and committed themselves to the mission.

He dedicated himself to the work and led the project with courage and determination.

God blessed his mission and it was successfully completed.

21
TRANSFORMATIONAL FOCUS

In the book of John chapter five, there was a scene that was very pathetic. It would have made any hospice, infirmary, nursing home, or hospital look like a vacation home. In Jerusalem, by the sheep gate, there was a pool called Bethesda, which in Hebrew meant House of Mercy. The pool had five porches and a great multitude of impotent, blind, lame, and sick folk lay on those porches on mats or beds and some just on the cold stone.

The interesting thing about this is that they were not only just lying there, but they were waiting for a strange phenomenon. It was the belief that an angel visited the pool at a certain time and stirred the water and whoever stepped in to the pool first after the stirring of the water was healed of whatever disease they had.

In this great multitude, there was a man who had been paralyzed for thirty-eight years. It is not clear if he had been at Bethesda for all those years but he had been there for a long time. There is no record about this man and his background or how he got to the pool, or the circumstance surrounding his crippled state. However, it is obvious that he, like the rest, was waiting for the stirring of the water so that he could get an opportunity to step in and get well.

There was a Jewish Feast and it was also the Sabbath day so Jesus was at Jerusalem celebrating the feast and visited the pool at Bethesda. Of all the people in the crowd, this one man stood out to him and He knew he had been in his condition for a long time and that he had been trying everything possible to get healed. Jesus approached the man and asked him a question which, on the surface, didn't make sense. In fact, it sounded very much like a cruel joke to ask a man who is crippled if he was willing to be made whole. However, on closer examination, Jesus never asked him if he was willing to be healed, for that was obvious. He asked him a deeper, far-reaching question which had to do more with his total self than his physical situation.

The question was if he was ready for not just healing but wholeness and if he was prepared to do whatever it took to be whole. Jesus knew that being whole involved a lot more than being healed and it was going to require a radical shift in this man's entire life.

It meant that every part of his being was going to be touched. His belief system was going to be shattered, and he was going to experience a transformation at the very core of his being. He was more in need of wholeness than healing and it was possible that he could have been healed but not made whole. When the process of wholeness takes place, it brings total wellness to the person who receives it.

The man did not fully understand the question and thought Jesus was just talking about his crippled condition. He gave a response which to him, seemed like a justified answer to his situation and lack of wholeness. He gave three reasons for his dilemma:

No help—I have no man to help me

No hope—I can't get into the pool

No strength—Others are more agile and empowered than I am

This response highlighted the man's true condition and his need for wholeness and why Jesus's question was so relevant and on target. He was not just crippled in his legs but he was suffering from other things that included a dependency syndrome where he was looking for a man to help. He also had a gimmicks mentality and his hope was in the angel stirring the water. There was a false sense of security for he believed that once he got in the pool everything would be OK. It is obvious that he was unable to move or act, but really it was mental paralysis and he suggested that he was at a competitive disadvantage because other folks were doing better than he was.

There were all these people who believed in the power of the pool to heal them but couldn't get into the pool, and there were others who took advantage of their disability with promises to help them into the pool—at a price. Jesus never offered any assistance to this man to get him into the pool and did not mention the angel or the pool for He knew the solution to this man's dilemma was not in a man, it was not in an angel, and certainly, it was not in the pool. The answer lay in the man's own ability to rise, take up his bed, and walk.

We often hear the saying "God helps those who help themselves." Although it is often quoted as Scripture, it is not in the Bible. However, there are many instances where it is implied as it is in this case. Jesus was not going to do for this man what he could do for himself.

The angel's visits to the pool were seasonal and unplanned and the angel just came and stirred the water but he never assisted anyone to get in. His action had no direct bearing on the man and there were no guarantees, so the answer was not in the angel.

The solution that Jesus gave lay within the ability of this man to reach inside himself and make it happen. Jesus invited him to do three simple things that he had the power to do but he also had to be willing.

The first thing Jesus said to him was "arise." That seemed like a dumb thing to say to a crippled man but Jesus was speaking to him from a different perspective and He was telling him to allow his mind to arise. The man's condition was not just physical but mental and Jesus was urging him to think clearly, positively and independently. There were barriers that needed to be dismantled and walls that had to be torn down as he was suffering from mental paralysis. He had a needy attitude and was looking for a quick fix so Jesus had to challenge him to allow his spirit to arise.

When you are in the same condition for thirty-eight years, your spirit will get down and it results in hopelessness, depression, self-defeating behavior, and an inferiority complex. Jesus was also telling him to let his faith arise. He had to redirect his faith away from the things he had trusted in for so long and place his faith in the words of Jesus and his own ability to rise.

The second command of Jesus was for him to take up his bed. The bed was one of the main contributing factors to his condition. What might have seemed as an asset to his well-being was an obstacle to his wholeness. Why rise when it is easier and more comfortable to lie down? The bed was limiting his ability to step up and step out and it was also time for him to carry that which had been carrying him. The bed represented safety, security, and ease and Jesus was asking him to step out of his comfort zone and take some risks.

By taking up his bed, he was taking responsibility for his destiny and it was not going to be in the hands of the man who would carry him into the water. It was also not the angel who would stir the water, or the pool that possessed the healing power for it was in his hands and he had to take it up.

Jesus gave him the third command and that was to walk. If you think the other commands were ridiculous, this one was over the top because the man had not walked for thirty-eight years. The people around him had told him he would never walk again, and he himself was resigned to the belief that he would not walk again but that he would die in that condition. When

Jesus told him to walk, He did not mean for him to take a few steps and test his ability to walk. He was commanding him to walk away from there, as Bethesda was a place for lame, impotent, and crippled folks. Jesus was saying "you are now whole; walk away not only from your old past but your old place. Bethesda is not conducive to your new consciousness and your new life."

He was also telling him to walk over his obstacles. Through the years, he had been walked upon and trampled by the crowd in their mad dash to get into the pool. He was now going to walk over all that was standing in his way of moving forward. I can just imagine hearing him asking people to excuse him as he stepped through the crowd.

His last command to him was to keep walking and never stop until he got to his destiny. Now he was walking away from the pool and into a new place.

Nehemiah had to help the people into transformation focus as they were in the same condition as this man and the entire nation needed wholeness and a sense of well-being. The job of a leader is to help the people they lead, to find that new place of peace, power, and prosperity and to get them to be people who can walk into their destiny.

22
VISION AND OUTCOMES

Vision requires that you to not only see what's ahead in the future but also what is around you and how those things may affect you and your mission. You may be focused on the things that you really think must be done right away and give them high priority. Placing them in the category of the urgent may be fine, as they must get done. The thing that you must not forget is that you cannot only focus on that which must be done here and now but also on that which you MUST NOT do. The vision plan states all the things that must get done and by what date and time. However, is there a section for the things that should not be done?

Nehemiah was very clear about his mission and he had a vision for what he wanted to see accomplished with the building of the wall and the restoration of the city. He also understood and knew very well the things that were not part of the mission that were going to be a distraction and not beneficial to the project.

The men who were in strong opposition to his rebuilding project made it clear that they were not pleased with his efforts and they were going to do whatever was possible to stop the project. Nehemiah stood up to them, encouraged his people in their rebuilding project, and they kept right on with their tasks. The wall was being built despite the threats and hostile environment and when the enemies saw that their plans were failing, they resorted to another scheme and pretended to now support the project. They invited Nehemiah to a meeting in one of the villages to discuss a report that had been circulating about the project. He replied that he was carrying on a great project and could not attend their meeting but they were persistent and sent four different invitations for meetings. Each time, he declined and refused to meet with them.

Vision allows you to see what is important and what is not and helps you prioritize and put in order what matters most. Nehemiah was aware of this and kept going about his business and doing that which needed to be done. He had the rebuilding of the wall as his primary focus and everything else was secondary. He had not come to Jerusalem to attend meetings and get involved in things that did not relate to his purpose and mission. Vision will keep you focused on your mission. It will also help you understand the true meaning of the mission and keep you in alignment with your calling. It causes you to constantly question what you are doing, why you're doing it and if it will result in the fulfillment of your mission.

When he stated that he was involved in a great project, it reinforced in his mind the real reason for him being there. He was strong in his conviction about the purpose for his mission. He had already established that there was nothing else that would merit leaving his project and he was determined to stay on the task that was given to him and see it to completion.

There are some important leadership lessons to learn from Nehemiah's approach:

1. You must constantly ask what is the work you are called to do and is this the place where you are called to work? This will help you to organize your work and ministry in such a way that you operate in the context of your calling and mission. The things you do now, the time you spend doing them and the effort you put into the tasks and responsibilities will help to ensure successful outcomes.

2. The goals and direction you set will help determine where your ministry or organization will be one to three years from now and will help to determine the scope and scale as well as the impact.

3. You must examine what external factors are influencing the progress of your mission and set ground rules that define what relationships are beneficial and those that are not.

4. There must be a clear outline of your roles and responsibilities and how you will go about doing them as this will help you stay on task and on message.

5. It is important to have a list of project items that must be accomplished as this will help you to be like Nehemiah. When you look at the list and see the number of things needed to be completed in the small amount of time, you will have to prioritize what gets done and be able to say to the detractors— I am doing a great work.

6. You must be resolved in your mind that it's OK to say no and not feel guilty for not attending every meeting or function you're invited to. You must have discernment to know what you need to do in those situations

7. Always pray for God to give you wisdom and the ability to perceive motives and intentions. Remember that you can only see the outside but God always sees the heart. This will save you from a lot of heartache and misery.

The enemies then changed their evil plan and devised another plot to get Nehemiah off track by suggesting that he go to the temple and shut the doors to hide from a fabricated death threat they had made up. He responded as a man on a mission and asked why he should run away even in the face of impending danger? Vision and mission will cause you to stare down the enemy and respond by answering that even though you walk through the valley of the shadow of death, you will fear no evil. He gave them a firm and resounding answer — "I will not go!"

He went on to observe that the men who had brought the message was not sent by God but had been hired by his adversaries. Their intention was to intimidate him and get him into a weak position and transgress against the laws of God so that he would receive a bad name and be discredited.

Vision enables us to have discernment to see not only what must be done but also what should be avoided. There are times we are on the right path, doing the right things and it is at that point that the enemy brings things our way to distract us. He wants to get us off course and may even result in us ending our mission. Remember that is his goal.

PART 3: PASSION

23
PAIN AND PASSION

Nehemiah was now faced with a dilemma. He had come to the city with a mission in mind, he had challenged the people, got them on board to help with the project and now the project was completed. The wall was built and the gates were back in place. However, there was a major problem happening. The collapse of the wall and the destruction of the city gates resulted in a breakdown of the normal everyday lives of the citizens.

The people could not get enough grain to grow or feed their families and they were mortgaging their fields, vineyards, and homes to get grain. They had to borrow money to pay the taxes on the land and the interest on those loans was extremely high. Things got so bad that they had to give over their children to slavery. They felt helpless and powerless and did not know how to handle the situation.

Word got to Nehemiah about what was happening and when he got the full story, he was very angry. He gathered the facts and called a town hall meeting with all concerned to sort out what was going on. This was not just a dispute between neighbors because the city officials, nobles, and priests were all involved. He realized that he could not just pray away this issue or hope that someone else would intervene and resolve the problem.

The people looked to him for leadership through the building project and they were now turning to him once again for guidance in this situation. Once you are perceived as a proven leader, people look to you for leadership in their times of difficulty. Missionaries do not get one assignment, complete the job and go home. I mentioned earlier about the British missionaries who were all things to all men in my island. Nehemiah was now beginning to understand that although he had taken leave from the palace and had given the king an estimated time of return, there was a situation that needed to be addressed. He could not walk away and leave it to be worked out by itself. All around us, there are tough problems that arise where we must figure out ways to address them and find answers.

Jesus and the disciples were out ministering to the people and it was a long day for the crowd that had gathered to hear Jesus teach. The disciples came to Jesus and told Him that the people had been there all day and they were now hungry and He should send them away so they could get food. Jesus turned to the disciples and told them that they should find food and feed the multitude. Jesus is saying the same thing to us when we mention in our prayer requests at church about all the things that are lacking in the community. He still turns to us and says — "you look around and come up with the answers to these problems." That's all in the work of missions. We are called to feed the hungry, clothe the naked, visit those in prison. When we do these things, we are doing it as part of our work as kingdom people to minister to those in need. We do it because it is the practical outworking of our faith.

Nehemiah stood up in the meeting and confronted the officials who were involved in extortion and land grabbing. He spoke out about what was happening and told them that what they were doing was wrong and they needed to stop it and he challenged them about walking in the fear of the Lord.

He insisted that they give back the lands and houses that they had seized and return the excessive taxes. Nehemiah spoke from his heart with passion and conviction and God spoke to the heart of the people who were involved in these unfair and unjust practices against their fellow Jews. The offenders agreed to stop the wicked practices, give back that which they had taken and not make any more unreasonable demands. He charged them to keep their promise and be true to the Lord their God. This was the beginning of a powerful reformation movement that was about to take over Jerusalem. Reformation takes place when people who know the will of God and understand His view of wrongdoing are willing to stand up and be the voice of God crying out against injustice and sin. When we confront unrighteousness in the power of the Holy Spirit, our God who is righteous, holy and hates wickedness will bring conviction to people's heart. We must be open and willing to allow Him to use us as His instruments and be a voice for Him. The leader must be willing to confront injustice. We can learn some lessons from Nehemiah and the early prophets and how they dealt with it.

The book of Isaiah has a great example:

> Surely the arm of the Lord is not too short to save, nor His ear too dull to hear. But your iniquities have separated you from your God; your sins have hidden His face from you, so that He will not hear.

> For your hands are stained with blood, your fingers with guilt. Your lips have spoken falsely, and your tongue mutters wicked things. No one calls for justice; no one pleads a case with integrity. They rely on empty arguments, they utter lies; they conceive trouble and give birth to evil.

> They hatch the eggs of vipers and spin a spider's web. Whoever eats their eggs will die, and when one is broken, an adder is hatched. Their cobwebs are useless for clothing; they cannot cover themselves with what they make. Their deeds are evil deeds, and acts of violence are in their hands.

> Their feet rush into sin; they are swift to shed innocent blood. They pursue evil schemes; acts of violence mark their

ways. The way of peace they do not know; there is no justice in their paths. They have turned them into crooked roads; no one who walks along them will know peace.

So, justice is far from us, and righteousness does not reach us. We look for light, but all is darkness; for brightness, but we walk in deep shadows. Like the blind we grope along the wall, feeling our way like people without eyes. At midday, we stumble as if it were twilight; among the strong, we are like the dead.

We all growl like bears; we moan mournfully like doves. We look for justice, but find none; for deliverance, but it is far away. For our offenses are many in your sight, and our sins testify against us. Our offenses are ever with us, and we acknowledge our iniquities, rebellion and treachery against the Lord, turning our backs on our God, inciting revolt and oppression, uttering lies our hearts have conceived.

So, justice is driven back, and righteousness stands at a distance; truth has stumbled in the streets, honesty cannot enter. Truth is nowhere to be found, and whoever shuns evil becomes a prey.

The Lord looked and was displeased that there was no justice.

He saw that there was no one, He was appalled that there was no one to intervene; so, His own arm achieved salvation for Him, and His own righteousness sustained him.

He put on righteousness as His breastplate, and the helmet of salvation on His head; He put on the garments of vengeance and wrapped Himself in zeal as in a cloak.

According to what they have done, so will He repay wrath to His enemies and retribution to His foes; He will repay the islands their due.

From the west, people will fear the name of the Lord, and from the rising of the sun, they will revere His glory. For He will come like a pent-up flood that the breath of the Lord drives along.

"The Redeemer will come to Zion, to those in Jacob who repent of their sins," declares the Lord. (Isa. 59:1–19 NIV).

There are some takeaways that we can use as we encounter incidents of injustice in our mission work.

1. God can change people and He wants to save them from the condition they're in, but sin and iniquity hinder that process. You must speak to sin and challenge people to turn away from their sinful ways.

2. The situation was grave as the people were committing acts of violence, war, and murder were everywhere but there was no call for justice. The truth is that amidst all the chaos, God expects His prophets to cry out loudly.

3. In addition to the lack of justice, there was also an absence of truth and honesty and those who decided to live upright with integrity became a target. You must realize that when you stand up for justice and righteousness, you will be targeted and marked as an enemy. Perhaps, this is the reason for the apathy and indifference because nobody wants to become a prey. However, the time has come for the fearless leaders to stand up and lead with boldness and courage.

4. There is a sad description of people looking for light but instead, finding darkness, walking in deep shadows, groping like the blind, feeling their way without eyes. They were stumbling at midday like it was night time and the whole place was in total darkness. We often preach about Jesus being the light of the world. Here is a great opportunity to turn on His light and let it shine brightly in the place of sin and darkness.

David reminds us of the power of the word and its ability to shed light in the dark place - "The unfolding of your words gives light; it gives understanding to the simple (Ps. 119:130 NIV)." This is a great opportunity for the bearers of the light to let it shine brightly.

5. The Lord is observing all that is happening and He is displeased that there is no justice. God is not just up in Heaven looking down and does not care—the truth is, God is mad. We must have the same reaction to injustice and unrigh-teousness; we cannot be passive or neutral. We must always side with God and see it through His eyes for He is all knowing and He is not happy with the practice of sin.

6. He was appalled and shocked that when He looked for someone to intervene, there were no volunteers and nobody who would step up to the plate. This was a situation that needed capable, gifted, and dedicated people. They would be His voice, His light and His hands to deal with the state of depravity, but He could not find one person to send out on this important mission to help the situation

Here is His word to us in our times

You are the salt of the earth. But if the salt loses its saltiness, how can it be made salty again? It is no longer good for anything, except to be thrown out and trampled underfoot. You are the light of the world. A town built on a hill cannot be hidden.

Neither do people light a lamp and put it under a bowl. Instead they put it on its stand, and it gives light to everyone in the house.

In the same way, let your light shine before others, that they may see your good deeds and glorify your Father in heaven. (Matt. 5:13–16 NIV)

24
PASSION FOR REFORMATION

Nehemiah was now governor of Jerusalem and this was the best thing that could happen to the city. The man who had risked his life and reputation, sacrificed his career and put everything on the line, was now in charge of the affairs of the city. He got to the governor's mansion and found that it was rife with corruption as the former governors had placed a heavy burden on the people by taking large amounts of money, food, and wine. Their assistants were also in on the deal and they too, robbed and exploited the people.

Nehemiah came from a background where honesty, uprightness, and integrity were important not only in his personal life but also for the position he was in. As the king's cupbearer, he held a position of trust. The ancient monarchs ruled with iron fists and they were aware that their opponents were constantly seeking opportunities to dethrone or kill them. Since the king relied heavily on military might, it was difficult to overthrow him, so one of the easiest ways to kill him was to poison him. The cupbearer's job was to taste the wine before the king drank it. This was to ensure that there was a safety buffer between the cupbearer and the king and his life was literally in the cupbearer's hand. There could not be the least suspicion that the cupbearer was not reliable or trustworthy. Nehemiah had proven that he was loyal, upright and a man of integrity.

His time in the palace as a servant of the king had prepared him for his new role as governor of Jerusalem. Perhaps the same thing is happening in your life. The place you're now in is getting you ready for the place where you're going to go to. What you do, and how you do it now, will help to determine your future performance.

Nehemiah saw and understood what the previous governors did and how they operated. He could easily have said that this was a precedent that was already set and that he was just continuing the practices that were in place when he got there. That's probably what the ordinary person would have done, but Nehemiah was not ordinary. He was a missionary and a visionary and a man of passion. He discontinued the corrupt practices and brought in a new order to the office of the governor. He attributed this change to his reverence for God and even though he was governor, he was still God's man and was determined to do things God's way.

There is always a strong temptation when one assumes a position of power to abuse it because power has a large appetite and will consume everything in its path. It takes a lot of restraint and discipline to resist the urge to exploit authority and abuse the power given to you. Nehemiah served an authoritarian king and had seen and understood what power does. However, because his heart was surrendered to God, he understood that the demands were heavy on the people and decided to make things easier for them. When reform happens at the top and trickles down, it will have a profound effect on everyone. The results will be seen and felt and the world will be a better place because of you and your commitment to honesty and integrity. These choices do not come easily. They are intentional, practiced and nurtured and eventually become a way of life.

Everywhere Nehemiah served, he impacted the place and made a difference in the lives of those around him. There are some very clear lessons that leaders must follow if they are going to be not just a person with a title, but someone people will follow. Their work and ministry will be a blessing to all.

> A leader must not be selfish and Nehemiah was a great example of an unselfish leader. Do nothing out of selfish ambition or vain conceit. Rather, in humility value others above yourselves (Phil. 2:3 NIV).

> Greatness is not in a title or position but rather in a heart that is contrite and humble. God wants you to be a servant-leader - Not so with you. Instead, whoever wants to become great

among you must be your servant (Matt. 20:26 NIV).

Righteousness is one of the main characteristics of a leader. The ministry must be built on righteousness - Kings detest wrongdoing, for a throne is established through righteousness (Prov. 16:12 NIV).

David had a great combination as a leader, which should be the goal of all leaders - And David shepherded them with integrity of heart; with skillful hands, he led them (Ps. 78:72 NIV).

25

PASSION FOR TRANSFORMATION

Many times, in the reformation process, it becomes necessary not only to confront and seek a just resolution but you will also have to take matters into your hands. Change and transformation is not always a nice and clean experience. It gets rough and dirty sometimes and you have to be willing to get into areas that require tough mental fortitude and deep spiritual conviction.

As the city of Jerusalem progressed and the city of Jerusalem was moving forward, there was an incident that involved the priest who was also the overseer of the storerooms in the temple. This priest developed a close association with one of the men who were in opposition to the rebuilding project and had caused major problems for Nehemiah and the people. The priest provided this man with a large room in the temple. It was a room to be used as a storage area for the grain offerings, incense, wine, olive oil, and other temple items that were designated for the Levites. This was a huge violation as this man was considered an enemy of the people of God and here he was, being provided accommodations in the house of God. He had fought against everything that was of God. He was not a part of what God was doing in the reformation movement that was happening in Jerusalem yet he was allowed into the temple and given a prominent place with the things of God.

One of Satan's schemes has always been to infiltrate the body of believers with imposters who present themselves as part of the flock but, they are devouring wolves that come to steal, kill, and destroy. As Christians in our various churches and groups, we should be welcoming people of different social and ethnic backgrounds and be open for newcomers and visitors to join in fellowship with us. However, spiritual leaders should be discerning and vigilant as shepherds of God's flock. They should not allow people who promote bigotry, evil, and violence to have access and exposure to the house of God and the people of God and be given prominent positions. This is indeed dangerous as corruption must never be entertained or condoned in any way and there must not be any perception of collusion and collaboration with people who are not for the things of God. Paul, in his writings to the Corinthians, rebuked them for their corrupt practices and warned them that God was not pleased with their behavior. Spiritual leaders must guard the house of God and not be partners in anything that is not pleasing to God.

Nehemiah had returned to his former service with the king and was not present while this was happening in Jerusalem. He later came back to Jerusalem and heard about what the priest had done in providing this man with a room in the temple. He was very angry with the situation and immediately went to the temple and threw out all his possessions and ordered that the room be cleansed and purified. He then put back the grain, oil, and incense that had been in the room previously. He was not going to tolerate the enemy of God occupying the house of God and he was very serious about the protection and integrity of the things of God. He did what God expected him to do and was not afraid to take a stand against the practice of evil and unrighteousness.

For true change and transformation to become a reality, all evil associations must be broken. The remnants of sin and wickedness must be removed and eradicated and you must ensure that the temple of God in you is purified and sanctified.

Leaders should be held to a high standard and they should separate themselves from evil and corruption. Failure to do so, will bring the judgment of God. Below are some verses that will help you to see this.

> Her priests do violence to my law and profane my holy things. They do not distinguish between the holy and the common. They teach that there is no difference between the unclean and the clean; and they shut their eyes to the keeping of my Sabbaths, so that I am profaned among them. Her officials within her are like wolves tearing their prey; they shed blood and kill people to make unjust gain. Her prophets

whitewash these deeds for them by false visions and lying divinations. They say, "This is what the Sovereign Lord says"—when the Lord has not spoken.

The people of the land practice extortion and commit robbery; they oppress the poor and needy and mistreat the foreigner, denying them justice. I looked for someone among them who would build up the wall and stand before me in the gap on behalf of the land so I would not have to destroy it, but I found no one. So, I will pour out my wrath on them and consume them with my fiery anger, bringing down on their own heads all they have done, declares the Sovereign Lord. (Ezek. 22:26–31 NIV)

Spiritual leaders are shepherds who are entrusted with feeding and taking care of the flock of God. They will be accountable for their service to the people they are responsible for caring

To the elders among you, I appeal as a fellow elder and a witness of Christ's sufferings who also will share in the glory to be revealed. Be shepherds of God's flock that is under your care, watching over them—not because you must, but because you are willing, as God wants you to be; not pursuing dishonest gain, but eager to serve; not lording it over those entrusted to you, but being examples to the flock. And when the Chief Shepherd appears, you will receive the crown of glory that will never fade away. (1 Pet. 5:1–4 NIV)

26
RESHAPING
THE MOVEMENT

When the Jews returned to the Promised Land, led by Joshua, eleven of the twelve tribes were allocated various portions of the land according to their size and rank. The tribe of Levi however, did not have an assigned territory and was not given an area for building homes or having a leadership structure. God had designated the Levites as His special, called-out tribe that was to be the priestly line, dedicating themselves to the service of the Lord. The other tribes were instructed to support them in their priestly service by giving them portions of all the produce of their fields as well as other offerings. The Levites only job was to serve in the temple and minister to the people and this principle was set by God and adhered to by the people as standard practice.

During the time of the breakdown of the wall, the ministry of the temple had ceased and the portions that were to be assigned to the Levites were not being given. They went back to the fields to work and provide for themselves. Since the Levites were in the fields working, there was no ministry going on in the temple.

This came to Nehemiah's attention and he called a meeting of the officials to find out what was going on. He got to the bottom of the situation and fixed the problem. The people started bringing tithes of grain, wine, and oil once again. Nehemiah set up an accountability structure by appointing a committee of trustworthy men along with assistants. He gave them the responsibility for the oversight of the storerooms and the distribution of the supplies to the Levites.

Things were back in order and the Levites resumed their service in the temple. Organization and structure are very important for the successful work of the ministry. When all areas are working, things will go smoothly and God will be glorified.

There was another problem area in the city that needed to be addressed. One of the commandments that God had given to the people through Moses at Mt. Sinai, was for them to remember the Sabbath day by keeping it holy. No work was to be done and all trading and commercial activity were to cease during that period.

However, Nehemiah observed that people were operating their winepresses and loading their donkeys with wine, grapes, figs, and other produce on the Sabbath. There were merchants from other places that were bringing in fish and other merchandise and selling them in Jerusalem to the people. The Sabbath, which was considered a day for rest and worship, was now turned into one of the biggest days of trading.

Nehemiah the reformer was on the job again. He had to call another meeting with the city officials to find out what was happening and why the Sabbath day was being desecrated. He challenged them about the practice and decided to impose restrictions that would curb all buying and selling on the Sabbath. He ordered that the city gates be closed on the evening before the Sabbath and that they would not reopen until the Sabbath was over. To ensure that this order was enforced, he assigned guards at the gates so no one could bring in any goods for sale. However, there were a few merchants who spent the night by the wall waiting to cash in, as all good merchants do. Nehemiah posted a notice warning all offenders that they could be arrested if they persisted in this practice. They heeded the warning and no longer gathered at the wall. The Levites, who were the guardians of the law, also got involved in helping to keep the Sabbath day holy for Nehemiah had commanded them to guard the gates.

Nehemiah was very passionate about his calling. He was dedicated to his work and committed himself to the reformation of the city. Whatever it took, he was going to do it. His goal was to transform the culture.

There was another issue that he felt needed attention and some resolution. The men of Jerusalem were marrying foreign women and it created not only cultural confusion but had resulted in an identity crisis for the children who were produced in these marriages. God had already warned them about marrying people from idol-worshipping nations as they would influence them in their heathen practices and lifestyles and eventually draw them away from their worship and reverence of the true and living God.

Many of the men did not heed the warnings and Nehemiah was so fired up about it that he lost his cool and yelled and screamed at them, beat them, and even pulled out their hair. He reminded them about Solomon who married foreign women and that they were instrumental in leading him astray into sinful behavior and lifestyles. He highlighted the example of the grandson of the high priest who was married to the daughter of the same man who was a foreigner and had openly opposed the building of the wall. He came from a priestly line but was connected to the heathen ways and culture. Nehemiah was so disgusted with him that he drove him away.

When a person is passionate about the things of God and the people of God, they will do whatever it takes to see God's will be established. Kingdom people are passionate people.

27
DESIRE AND PASSION FOR THE WORD

After the wall was rebuilt, the people settled in their various towns and things were getting back to normal. However, there was still one thing that was missing. There had not been a time of gathering for corporate worship since the wall was destroyed and they had not been able to hear the word of God. At that time, they had no Bibles like we have today so they went to the temple to hear the word read by the priests. There was a time when they gathered often and heard the word read and got inspired. However, it had been quite a while and they were longing to hear the word once again

Imagine if your city was hit by a storm and your place of worship was destroyed so you could not gather for worship and fellowship. That would impact your life greatly, especially if you're accustomed to attending the various services along with friends and relatives that you would usually have fellowship with. If that were taken away, it would leave you with a longing to meet and have fellowship with the saints. There is something about corporate worship that uplifts you and helps in your Christian walk. Gathering together makes you stronger.

There was a hunger to hear the word of God being read. On this day, all the people gathered in the town square to listen to Ezra, the senior priest, read from the word of God. He stood up on a raised wooden platform, accompanied by the priests and assistants and read the book from early dawn until noon while the people listened attentively. Ezra opened the book and began to praise God. The people responded in affirmation with their hands raised and fell to their knees and worshipped God with their faces to the ground. There was a heavy presence of the Spirit of God in the gathering and the people were just absorbed in the word and worship.

As Ezra read, his assistants explained what was being read so the people could understand. They all stood and listened to everything attentively. Nehemiah and the Levites also joined in the teaching of the word. They exhorted the people to be joyful and give praise to God because they were weeping as they heard the words being read. It was truly an emotional experience since they had not heard the word for quite some time and it moved them.

The leaders encouraged the people to go home and have a time of feasting, eating and drinking, and enjoying the good things that God had done for them. They were also instructed to include the poor in their celebration and share the blessings with those who did not have enough. When God moves our spirits, He also moves our hearts to generosity and sharing. This is a response to the goodness of God to us, and as He blesses us we should pass the blessings on to those in need.

The word began to take root in their hearts as they got an understanding of what was being read to them. They returned on the second day to hear the word again and to dig deeper and find greater meaning to all that was in the book. They discovered some wonderful truths and began to act on it and celebrate the blessings of God. They held a solemn assembly and gathered for a time of mourning and repentance. After a long pause in the worship in the temple, the word was now having a prominent place in the hearts of the people and in the heart of the nation. Whenever the word of God goes forth in power and might, things will never be the same. The word brings transformation and things will change when the truth of the word is received, for it will make a difference.

There is no substitution for the word of God being read in gatherings and corporate worship but more importantly in your personal devotional time. The people in Nehemiah's day could only hear the word read when they went to the temple because they did not have a personal copy of the word of God as it is today. They depended on the priest to read it to them and it was only at appointed times when they gathered for temple worship.

The reading of the word of God allows you to hear from God and understand His will for your life. I would encourage everyone to begin a daily habit of reading the word of God at a time that's fit for your schedule and let it become a regular practice. As you read the Bible, you will begin to experience a transformation in your personal and family life and it will also affect your professional life.

The passion for the word will also result in a passion for holy living. When the word of God is applied in your heart, it penetrates the areas of sinfulness. It will drive out the wickedness from your life and give you a desire to serve God and to do the things that God requires.

Reading the word also brings peace and calm in this world of chaos and confusion. You can find the promises of God for provision and protection. As you rest on those promises, you will see that God always fulfills His promises and He will do what He says and be true to His word.

28
RESPONSE AND REACTION TO THE WORD

The reading of the word was no longer just a ceremonial exercise and it began to take effect in the hearts and lives of the people. They broke off all relations with foreigners, confessed their sins and the iniquities of their fathers. They worshipped and cried out to God in loud voices. They acknowledged Him as the Creator and Sustainer who demonstrated His goodness by bringing their forefather Abraham out from Ur of the Chaldees and making a covenant with him. They remembered His deliverance in bringing their ancestors out of Egypt. They recalled how He took them through the wilderness, providing them with food and shelter on their journey. They went on to recite how God fought for His people, protected them from their enemies and rescued them from the hands of those who sought to destroy them.

They recounted the disobedience and rebellion of their forefathers despite all that God had done for them. How they were turned over to their enemies who made their lives miserable but each time God heard and answered their cries for mercy and turned things around in their favor. As they prayed, they repented and confessed to God that He had done everything right and it was they who were wrong. They agreed that they too were now in a situation where they were equal to slaves. The crops they harvested, had been taken by the rulers who could do whatever they chose with them because they were their servants. They concluded that they were in deep trouble and they were going to draw up a binding document pledging to be true and obedient to God. They would have their leaders sign it on behalf of the people to hold them all accountable.

Something is wrong when people hear the word of God over and over and time after time and yet they are unresponsive to it. The old saints back in the church where I grew up referred to this condition as being "gospel hardened." This meant that the person, after hearing the word repeatedly, had become immune to it and it did not move them. The premise for that comes from the book of Hebrews where it states, "Today if you hear His voice, do not harden your hearts as you did in the rebellion (Heb. 3:15 NIV)."

Their ancestors heard the word and were disobedient to it and rebelled against it. They knew the conse-quences of those actions and having seen the results, ultimately decided not to go that route. The response to the word of God was far-reaching and it affected them in three ways so they all pledged that:

Lifestyle

They would follow the Law of God and carefully obey all the commands, regulations and decrees of the Lord.

There would be no more mixed marriages and they would refrain from marrying people who were not committed to God.

They would give the land a break every seventh year and not plant any crops in that year.

Financial

They would not engage in buying, selling, trading, or any form of merchandising on the Sabbath.

They would give a tithe of the crop to the Levites.

The people who were owed money would cancel all debts that were owed to them.

Worship

They would give one-third of a shekel per year to the service of the house of God.

They would bring the first fruits of the crops of every fruit tree to the house of the Lord.

Each family would bring wood to burn on the altar at the time that was determined.

They would not neglect the House of God.

It is possible that in many churches today, people have been going to church for a long time but they are just hearers of the word and not doers of the word so it has no effect on their lives. They keep on living the same way with no change for all the years they've been in church. Jesus gives some very clear requirements for people who desire to follow Him and become His disciples:

Then He said to them all: "Whoever wants to be my disciple must deny themselves and take up their cross daily and follow me. For whoever wants to save their life will lose it, but whoever loses their life for me will save it. What good is it for someone to gain the whole world, and yet lose or forfeit their very self? Whoever is ashamed of me and my words, the Son of Man will be ashamed of them when He comes in His glory and in the glory of the Father and of the holy angels." (Luke 9:23–26 NIV)

If you are going to be a true follower of Jesus, you must allow Him to lead and be your guide. Following Jesus involves giving up your will and submitting to His will. It will require you to embrace suffering and hardship so that you may share in His glory. He calls His followers to a life of self-sacrifice and self-denial and total surrender to His Lordship. He asks that you give up all your worldly desires and personal ambitions to live a life that is pleasing and acceptable to Him.

He wants you to get to the place where you are willing to let go of the things that you consider important so that He can give you the things that are far more valuable. He offers you real peace, joy, and satisfaction to replace the things you hold on to that are fake, phony, and temporal. If you are embarrassed to live this way and instead please yourself and others, when He returns in His glory He will be embarrassed with you.

This is Jesus's call to true discipleship and your response to His word will be the deciding factor to the quality of your life. The people in Jerusalem decided to follow the word of the Lord.

29
REVIVAL AND REVITALIZATION

Revival had come to Jerusalem! After a period of spiritual inactivity and moral decline, the power of God was now at work in the lives of the people once again.

They had fallen to a very low point in their spiritual experience and as a result, the society was broken and the people had lost their way. Nehemiah came to build the city walls but also discovered that there was a lot of rebuilding to do in the lives of the people.

The issues that arose were symptoms of a people who had gone astray from God and no longer followed His commands. There was no spiritual leadership or guidance and because the laws of God were no longer important to them, they became a lawless society. There were no absolutes and whatever seemed good to them, they just did it. They were motivated by greed, and injustice was everywhere.

God was not through with His people and He put it in the heart of Nehemiah to go to Jerusalem to start a building project. This resulted in opening avenues for growth and prosperity in the nation as well as spiritual renewal and revival. There were a lot of issues that needed to be addressed and Nehemiah was bold, and willing to confront them. In his initial prayer, when he got the news of the situation, he sensed that there was a serious breakdown. However, when he got to the city, he had the confirmation of what was already in his mind. He realized that it was at a greater proportion than he anticipated.

> He had the courage to go to Jerusalem and brought with him the experience he had gained in the palace as the cupbearer. He also brought the same characteristics of honesty and loyalty to the project in Jerusalem. He served alongside the people with integrity and honor even when it was risky and dangerous to serve.

> He learned how to overcome evil and wickedness and push through in the face of real and present danger. He also had to learn how to resolve conflicts, solve problems, and make life-changing decisions.

> He guided the people and showed them the power of faith over unbelief. The power of ability over helplessness. The power of self-determination over the hopelessness of being dominated by rulers who had taken advantage of them for many years.

The people now had the ability and courage to live life as God intended it, rather than continuing to live in despair and despondency. Nehemiah helped them to understand that the real key to living was to put their trust in God and to always follow His commands.

Together with the people, he worked on tough problems even when they seemed to be beyond his ability. He eventually took on increasingly greater responsibilities and with the help of Almighty God, got to the point of completing the building project and experiencing a complete turnaround of the city. This helped to point the Jewish people toward a brighter future. He had the joy of seeing them work independently and in cooperative groups as they gave of themselves wholeheartedly and offered their skills and abilities to help build the wall.

Revival is not about a visiting evangelist coming to town, or a series of gospel meetings scheduled on the church's calendar. Revival results in change and transformation. People's hearts and minds are touched. Cities are transformed and strongholds are broken. Places that once were in darkness shine again with the light of Christ and true repentance is evident. Revival is not just singing, shouting and clapping of the hands, but rather a mighty moving of the Spirit of God among the people of God.

When revival comes, sinners will come to the altar, cry out to God, repent of their sins, and turn from their evil ways. The power of Almighty God comes like a tidal surge that washes away bitterness, anger, hatred, and fear. People who were sick get healed. People who were weak, become strong. Those who lack, experience abundance. In a revival season, people are delivered and chains are broken. There is an atmosphere of the supernatural and you will know that God has visited His people.

30
HERE WE ARE

The people put together a pledge and had the rulers sign it. They committed to giving annual offerings to the temple consisting of the first fruits of their crops and the firstborn of their herds and flock. They decided to give the best of the grain, contributions of fruit, wine, and oil to the priests. They also promised a tithe from the produce of their fields to the Levites and they solemnly vowed that they would not neglect the temple of the Lord.

These commitments ensured that the work of God continued and the offerings assisted the Levites in the work of the temple. It also allowed the priests and musicians to serve. Ministry was now given priority and they saw it as vital to the nation's existence.

There is a direct connection between generosity, stewardship, effective ministry, and a thriving nation. When the people stopped giving their gifts, offerings, and tithes, the Levites and priests stopped receiving the provisions that were allotted to them for their ongoing support. Since they did not have any means of a livelihood, the priests went back to the fields to work so they could have food to eat and daily provisions. While they were in the fields, there was no ministry happening in the temple. Since the word of God was not going forth, and the people were not attending worship or prayer meetings, they began to live outside the will of God and the nation went into moral decline.

God designed the way that this was to work and when the people followed His plan, everything went well. When they became disobedient, things went out of alignment. For a ministry to be successful it must be supported by the people and they must ensure the sustainability of the ministry. As the ministry becomes more effective, it will have a greater impact on the society and everyone will be better off for it.

This was David's vision when he prayed in the Psalms

> Rid me, and deliver me from the hand of strange children, whose mouth speaketh vanity, and their right hand is a right hand of falsehood: That our sons may be as plants grown up in their youth; that our daughters may be as corner stones, polished after the similitude of a palace: That our garners may be full, affording all manner of store: that our sheep may bring forth thousands and ten thousands in our streets: That our oxen may be strong to labor; that there be no breaking in, nor going out; that there be no complaining in our streets. Happy is that people, that is in such a case: yea, happy is that people, whose God is the Lord. (Ps. 144:11–15 KJV)

Such a life is possible and it's what God wants for you but it does not happen by chance or accident. It is intentional and people must want it and be willing do what is necessary to achieve it. God intended for His people to be prosperous and He delights in giving good gifts. However, your heart must be open to give to the Lord generously, with a loving heart. There are guidelines in Scripture for giving to the Lord, seen below.

God wants you to give freely and willingly and your gifts should come from a joyful heart. When the people were withholding their gifts from the house of the Lord, they were in a state of despair and despondency. When they decided to give their tithes and offerings, God brought joy to their hearts and they could now give freely.

> "Each of you should give what you have decided in your heart to give, not reluc-tantly or under compulsion, for God loves a cheerful giver (2 Cor. 9:7 NIV)."

This is a fundamental principle and one that all should take heed to. The path to prosperity is not in a better job or increase in business. The Bible says that as you give and be generous, you will prosper. "A generous person will prosper; whoever refreshes others will be refreshed (Prov. 11:25 NIV)."

This is a great account of David and his people giving their gifts to the Lord for the building of the temple. The people rejoiced when they saw the leaders giving and it inspired them to give. They confessed that every-thing that they possessed came from the Lord and they were giving it back to Him for His use.

> Then King David said to the whole assembly: "My son Solomon, the one whom God has chosen, is young and inexperienced. The task is great, because this palatial structure is not for man but for the Lord God. With all my resources, I have provided for the temple of my God. Gold for the gold work, silver for the silver, bronze for the bronze, iron for the iron and wood for the wood, as well as onyx for the settings, turquoise, stones of various colors, and all kinds of fine stone and marble, all of these in large quantities.

> "Besides, in my devotion to the temple of my God I now give my personal trea-sures of gold and silver for the temple of my God, over and above everything I have provided for this holy temple: three thousand talents of gold and seven thousand talents of refined silver, for the overlaying of the walls of the buildings, for the gold work and the silver work, and for all the work to be done by the craftsmen. Now, who is willing to con-secrate themselves to the Lord today?"

Then the leaders of families, the officers of the tribes of Israel, the commanders of thousands and commanders of hundreds, and the officials in charge of the king's work gave willingly. They gave toward the work on the temple of God five thousand talents and ten thousand darics of gold, ten thousand talents of silver, eighteen thousand talents of bronze and a hundred thousand talents of iron.

Anyone who had precious stones gave them to the treasury of the temple of the Lord in the custody of Jehiel the Gershonite. The people rejoiced at the willing response of their leaders, for they had given freely and wholeheartedly to the Lord. David the king also rejoiced greatly. David praised the Lord in the presence of the whole assembly, saying, "Praise be to you, Lord, the God of our father Israel, from everlasting to everlasting.

"Yours, Lord, is the greatness and the power and the glory and the majesty and the splendor, for everything in heaven and earth is yours. Yours, Lord is the kingdom; you are exalted as head over all. Wealth and honor come from you; you are the ruler of all things. In your hands are strength and power to exalt and give strength to all. Now, our God, we give you thanks, and praise your glorious name. But who am I, and who are my people, that we should be able to give as generously as this? Everything comes from you, and we have given you only what comes from your hand." (1 Chron. 29:1–14 NIV)

When you give, it will come right back to you

Give, and it will be given to you. A good measure, pressed down, shaken together and running over, will be poured into your lap. For with the measure you use, it will be measured to you. (Luke 6:38 NIV)

You honor the Lord when you give

Honor the Lord with your wealth, with the first fruits of all your crops; then your barns will be filled to overflowing, and your vats will brim over with new wine. (Prov. 3:9–10 NIV)

God will enlarge your harvest and cause you to increase

There is no need for me to write to you about this service to the Lord's people. For I know your eagerness to help, and I have been boasting about it to the

Macedonians, telling them that since last year you in Achaia were ready to give; and your enthusiasm has stirred most of them to action. But I am sending the brothers in order that our boasting about you in this matter should not prove hollow, but that you may be ready, as I said you would be.

For if any Macedonians come with me and find you unprepared, we, not to say anything about you, would be ashamed of having been so confident. So, I thought it necessary to urge the brothers to visit you in advance and finish the arrangements for the generous gift you had promised. Then it will be ready as a generous gift, not as one grudgingly given. Remember this: Whoever sows sparingly will also reap sparingly, and whoever sows generously will also reap generously.

Each of you should give what you have decided in your heart to give, not reluctantly or under compulsion, for God loves a cheerful giver. And God is able to bless you abundantly, so that in all things at all times, having all that you need, you will abound in every good work. As it is written: "They have freely scattered their gifts to the poor; their righteousness endures forever."

Now he who supplies seed to the sower and bread for food will also supply and increase your store of seed and will enlarge the harvest of your righteousness. You will be enriched in every way so that you can be generous on every occasion, and through us your generosity will result in thanksgiving to God. This service that you perform is not only supplying the needs of the Lord's people but is also overflowing in many expressions of thanks to God. Because of the service by which you have proved yourselves, others will praise God for the obedience that accompanies your confession of the gospel of Christ, and for your generosity in sharing with them and with everyone else.

And in their prayers for you their hearts will go out to you, because of the surpassing grace God has given you. Thanks be to God for his indescribable gift! (2 Cor. 9: 1–15 NIV)

This is what the people were guilty of doing. They were withholding the tithes from the Levites but God says you must not be like them — "Do not withhold good from those to whom it is due, when it is in your power to act (Prov. 3:27 NIV)."

God promised that as you give to Him, He will protect your crops and fields and whatever you possess. God will take care of it

> "Bring the whole tithe into the store-house, that there may be food in my house. Test me in this," says the Lord Almighty, "and see if I will not throw open the floodgates of heaven and pour out so much blessing that there will not be room enough to store it. I will prevent pests from devouring your crops, and the vines in your fields will not drop their fruit before it is ripe," says the Lord Almighty. "Then all the nations will call you blessed, for yours will be a delightful land," says the Lord Almighty. (Mal 3:10–12 NIV)

31

A NEW OUTLOOK

There was a radical shift in the entire system in Jerusalem when the wall was broken down. The wall was the main structure of the nation and represented safety and prosperity. The destruction of the wall and the city gates caused everything else to be affected and there was a major change in the usual way of life. The practices and customs they once followed were disrupted and the pillars of the society were fractured. After the wall was rebuilt and the infrastructure restored, it was important to have the core institutions reinstated. The citizens needed to adjust to the emerging times that were so different from the past and adapt to a society that had changed significantly.

Most of the people who lived in the city were taken away as captives and those who escaped, ran off to other cities to start a new life. Nehemiah and the leaders encouraged the Jews that were in exile to return to the city. There were specific families that were targeted who could bring certain talents and contribute resources that would greatly help the reorganization of the city. Many of them returned to be a part of the reconstructed city and contribute to its growth and development. It was an enormous task and there was a lot to be done. Just like the group that was committed to building the wall and saw it completed, so these people were now dedicated to nation building and community transformation.

They came with a different mindset and were determined to see their city rise and grow again. They did their best to help ensure that it was not only safe and secure but that it was going to be peaceful and prosperous. They were very happy to see the city rebuilt but it was also now time for nation building and there was a lot to be done in this process. They were up to the task and were willing to do whatever it took to make it happen.

The time came for the dedication of the wall and all the people came together for a joyful celebration of what God had done and how He brought them through. The singers and musicians gathered on the wall and once again there was a sound of praise coming from the people. It was not just sounds of instruments and voices but it was a loud sound of people with grateful hearts, rejoicing and glorifying God for all He had done. There was a lot to be grateful for and they understood what it was to be truly thankful as they had a new perspective.

A thriving community that is growing and flourishing is vital for the ongoing well-being of the people who live there. They must be able to not only envision, but also experience the opportunities and the possibilities of today and tomorrow. It must be a place that offers hope and potential, and the results of their endeavors, determination and efforts must be seen and felt. This spirit inspires people to work together to build economic, infrastructural and social development. You must look at the issues that impact the direction of the community and seek to focus on positive influences. Every effort must be made to build unity, self-determination, competence, generosity, openness, and self-sacrifice.

When selfishness, greed, and injustice is embedded in the community, it will result in the erosion of the strength and confidence of the people. It also brings with it a spirit of disunity, suspicion, and fear. The breakdown of the peace and prosperity does not happen suddenly. There is a slow and silent shift of the standards and principles and it goes down over time. It is not easy to detect the fall as it is a slow-moving process that is not easily noticeable and increases over time.

As the situation develops, it is seen and felt but no one pays attention or acts on it for they think that all is well and it will eventually work out. Satan has a way of making people feel that it is OK and, even though they may feel that what they're doing is not right, they do nothing about it, thinking that the problem will go away. The erosion is so slow that people are generally not aware that what was once an abundant life has slowly turned into a new way of living in depravity and corruption. They have come to believe that it is just a little cultural shift and it is OK. In fact, while they are in this state of decline, they are also in a state of denial and do not realize the divisiveness, and hopelessness that have overtaken them. This may be the underlying cause of the economic and social problems in our communities. This condition needs to be changed with a new mindset and a spirit of godliness, integrity, caring, and love. There is a need to raise the values of the society and follow the principles that are in keeping with what God has laid out in His word.

The emphasis should be on developing progressive, dynamic, and prosperous communities that are great places to live, work, and play and display these outstanding features:

> Give respect and show kindness to all people. You must not allow differences in, politics, culture, religion, economics and race to overshadow your sense of compassion and caring. Demonstrate a spirit of openness and see beyond outward human differences and seek to become united in vision and purpose. Generosity and sharing must be the mark of kingdom people.

> Recognize that the knowledge and prosperity we need come from God and you must not be totally reliant on professionals to make it happen for you. There is a lot of wisdom in the people in your local communities and you must use their shared knowledge and resourcefulness to solve your problems

Trust in the unlimited power of Almighty God and you must believe that God is able to do exceedingly, abundantly above all you are able to ask, think or imagine. You must not allow modern thinking and philosophies to turn you from your inherent belief in God as the Supreme Being and the One who gives life and sustains life. You should always honor, worship and praise Him. You must also recognize that failure to do so will result in demise, as other nations before us.

Act on the belief that communities can be built from the strengths and talents of the local people and not from professionals only. Although you should welcome outside assistance, you must promote the abundance of talent and skills that is present in the community. The residents must be able to make a successful living in their communities and the goal of economic development is to help with job creation and viable, sustainable systems of support for all.

Encourage and teach the idea that when people work together and collaborate, they expand and enlarge their reach. When they join forces, it provides opportunities for new organizations with greater impact and influence.

The problems of the communities (crime, economics, and land development) can be addressed and solved through community outreach efforts.

Choose leaders who see that leadership is about being intentional, visionary, caring, building community, and being open and honest. They should understand that leadership is not about personality but that it requires integrity, moral fiber, and spiritual strength.

Develop a team of community workers who willingly serve in the vital role of caring services. These should be people who have a spirit of caring and are equipped and ready to serve and minister to the community. Caring people have the power of bringing people together and they find joy in linking, organizing, and getting people to unite. They contribute to a community's value by helping to increase the participation of people who would not normally get involved.

Recognize that the professionals can deliver services, but only when the people feel a strong sense of community and begin to care for each other, will true service be realized.

Build strong fellowship in your groups by elevating the quality of your meetings and that would help to create and develop friendships and unity among the members.

Revise the community emphasis with a vision that it is not about getting it right or becoming the biggest and best. It is about creating an environment of encouragement, gratefulness, and joyfulness.

Motivate your people and help to develop their skills and talents. Allow them to find their calling and perform to the best of their ability. This will help the community to develop and grow and change will be evident. Transformation will happen by the power of small groups of dedicated people.

These are some of the lessons that community and ministry leaders can utilize to help build active, strong, and progressive communities. There is a need for a greater emphasis on community building that will help stem the eroding impact of materialism and divisiveness that has become an integral part of many communities. To effectively respond to the negative forces on communities, Community Transformation must be at the heart of every initiative and should be integrated into and connected as an organized effort.

A transformation project, like that which Nehemiah initiated in Jerusalem, is needed today to shift people's consciousness to values and actions that are God centered. Such a movement can do a lot to get people back on track, bring God into focus again and constantly keeping the possibilities of a new community in the mind and vision of the residents. A new outlook will give purpose and meaning to communities and cities and those that are in need of revival and revitalization.

32
LOOKING TO
THE FUTURE

The people were now ready to follow God's plan for them and they were doing this, freely and willingly with a strong desire to please Him. Sometimes it takes severe circumstances for us to turn back to God and get in alignment with His will for our lives.

Growing up in the Caribbean islands where hurricanes and tropical storms are a way of life, I understood what it was like to go through a storm season. Each year, the hurricane center would send out a list of hurricane names and a forecast of what to expect during the hurricane season. They would remind you of the things that were necessary to prepare for them. I have experienced at least six major hurricanes in my lifetime and it was not pleasant, as they brought devastation and destruction. Storms have the power to destroy buildings and tear down walls. Because the islands are surrounded by oceans, the giant waves push inland and can wash away anything that is in its path. After the storm was over, the people came out to assess the damage and for those who lost property and possessions, it was very depressing.

However, if you came back in a few years and saw the areas that were affected, you would see new buildings that replaced the ones that were destroyed. The infrastructure and environment got a whole new makeover. One of the blessings was that the storm took away and removed stuff that should not have been there. Things that had become a problem were washed away and gone in the storm. New structures were built and things were back to order in a new and different way.

That is how it must have been in Jerusalem after the breaking down of the walls and the destruction of the city gates. The men who came to visit Nehemiah described it in very graphic terms. They told him the wall was still rubble and the city gates were cinders. Nehemiah grew up in the city and knew it very well and that description was far from what he knew of the city before it was burnt and broken. However, it had changed and there was a new reality.

Things around us may crumble and fall and the life we once knew can change dramatically in quick time. The real issue is not what happens in our lives but rather how we deal with the storms that will come. The only choice Nehemiah saw at that time was that the walls had to be rebuilt. He was not clear how it was going to happen and he did not have the means to do it, but he was certain that it had to be done.

Now that the wall was rebuilt and the gates were back in place, the project was completed but the real work of community building and ministry was just getting started. The people were now revived by the Spirit of God, reformation was happening, there was also a new awakening in the community. The building of the wall helped them to see the possibilities of what can happen when people pool their skills together and work in unity. They also experienced what it was like to live through a crisis period and overcome the fear of being attacked and persevere to finish the work despite the threats. They saw the protecting hand of God keeping them through times of danger, eventually delivering them from their enemies and the people who oppressed and mistreated them. They were now experiencing the provision of God as He was blessing their crops and causing the fields to produce an abundant harvest and they could provide for their families and pay their bills.

They had been through a lot and it was quite an interesting journey. They were now at a new place in their lives and the future was before them with all the wonderful possibilities and hope was once again restored. Jerusalem had become a thriving city and the citizens were living well and prospering. The desolation and despair that had overtaken the place were a distant memory and they were now free to go on with their lives.

Nehemiah introduced a new style of leadership. He had a different way of handling situations, solving problems and overcoming difficulties. They were committed to learning from the experiences and design a new path for moving forward. There were some important principles they learned along the way to their future:

Adversity comes at times to destroy the old institutions that are built on greed, corruption, and injustice. It opens new opportunities for spiritual growth, social justice, and infrastructural development. The society was now aware of the things that could go wrong but they also knew that what was broken could be rebuilt and restored.

Times of crisis can be a platform for great people who have leadership skills, to emerge. They must be willing to accept the call to mission. They must embrace the struggle, shoulder the burdens and lead people who are discouraged and in despair, to a place of hope and peace.

Broken walls and burnt gates are not the final state of the community. It is an occasion for redesigning and reshaping a system that might have been flawed and needed to be fixed and made right.

Periods of disaster can become defining moments that can change the course of life and produce the best fruit.

The process of rebuilding allowed them to strengthen not only the infrastructure but also skills, instincts abilities, resources, and organizations.

Having gone through the restoration of the wall and the re-establishment of the city, they now had a different mindset and a shifting perception of the community.

This was going to be a long-term and ongoing journey. The building process would not end with the completion of the wall, but it would be the beginning of a new era.

Through the struggles, a loving and caring community had been created that looked out for each other and this would be the model for the next generation to use as they continued in the work of community building.

Good leaders were now in place and the old guard had been removed so it was possible for new policies to be implemented that would be beneficial for all.

They could now share the lessons they learned from this project with other communities and help them to overcome similar problems that they may face.

These lessons from the book of Nehemiah are relevant for us today in the 21st century. Let us take heed to them and seek to become people of Mission, Vision and Passion.

ABOUT THE AUTHOR

R oy Benjamin has worked in several IT positions at various companies for the last twenty-one years. At his most recent assignment, he served as the Vision Leader and Chief Consultant for a start-up tech company in Atlanta.

He combines his wide-ranging technical expertise and broad understanding of multiple disciplines to help organizations. Roy also integrates his knowledge of products, services, and internal operations to help create successful outcomes. He has advised on various technology systems and procedures.

Roy has a background in outreach ministry, community development, and government. His employment experiences have included serving as National Director of Youth for Christ in the Caribbean island of St. Kitts, and Assistant to the Minister of Communications, Works and Public Utilities in the Federal Government of St. Kitts and Nevis.

Roy is passionate about Ministry Outreach and believes that churches and ministries must be mission oriented. He has developed a program called Community Outreach Systems to help them reach their communities. As a strong advocate of outreach to men, he is very involved in his church's men's Bible study.

He is a gifted speaker and a thought leader and has traveled extensively, speaking at various churches and events. He offers consultation services for Outreach Systems on many topics and issues. Go to roybenjamin.net to reach Roy for speaking or consultation

CPSIA information can be obtained
at www.ICGtesting.com
Printed in the USA
FSOW02n2300141017
39891FS

65510195R00082

Made in the USA
Lexington, KY
14 July 2017